The Green Door Cookbook

Published by: Rosetta Publications
                 The Green Door Restaurant
                 198 Main Street
                 Ottawa, Ontario, Canada K1S 1C6

Printed at
            : Tina and Company Print and Digital Reproduction, Ottawa

Cover
        : Footpath Design

Illustrations:
Jude Farmer: pages
Ron Farmer: pages : 17, 21, 28, 34, 36, 44, 52, 58, 74, 80, 100, 119, 133, 158
                    : 41, 43, 45, 51, 68, 70, 91, 95, 102, 127, 130, 151, 157

Photographs by Ron Farmer
Layout by Noah Farmer and Ron Farmer
Chefs d'Ordinateur: Noah Farmer and Ron Farmer

Canadian Cataloguing in Publication Data

Weaver, Poppy, 1942-
            The Green Door Cookbook

Includes Index
ISBN 978-0-9684639-0-1
            1. Vegetarian Cookery. 2. Green Door Restaurant
            1. Green Door Restaurant. 11.Title

TX837.W42 1998 641.5'636   C98-901415-0

First Printing: September 1999
Second Printing: December 1999
Third Printing: October 2001
Fourth Printing: December 2005, revised, with 13 additional recipes
Fifth Printing: March 2007
Sixth Printing: December 2007
Seventh Printing: February 2009
www.thegreendoor.ca

Dedication
This book is dedicated to the many customers of The Green Door, without whose interest, appreciation and support, this book may never have been written.

Acknowledgements

Special thanks to: Sheila Keene, Allison Berneche, and all the staff, past and present, of The Green Door Restaurant.

Introduction

This book was written in response to the numerous questions and requests by customers about the recipes, the creation of which has evolved from the authors' personal taste, knowledge, and cooking experiences over many years.

We developed recipes that use healthful whole grains, beans, nuts, seeds, sea vegetables, as well as fresh fruits and vegetables. The climate in this region of Canada allows approximately 100 frost-free days in any given year. Preference is given to local organic produce; the menu changes to embrace seasonal ingredients.

We draw on local resources throughout the year, from fiddleheads in the early spring to burdock roots and hardy greens, the last vegetables to be harvested in the late fall. The first jug of maple syrup, which may come as early as late February, is always greeted with excitement, and discussions follow as to how well and long the sap will flow and how it will affect the supply and price of the syrup in the following months. This is important to us because it is our sweetener of choice and we use approximately 300 gallons a year.

This approach to food not only promotes good health, but also supports local organic farmers, whose small-scale, often family-run farms are not profit-driven, but rather a labour of love.

Our methods of preparation are sometimes simple, at other times, elaborate. Almost everything is made from scratch, the old-fashioned way.

We start serving food at 11:00 AM. In the restaurant kitchen, however, the day starts at six. The aroma of the sourdough rising in large bowls fills the bakery. The cook in charge of the day's menu will check supplies before making final menu decisions. Could any newly arrived treasures inspire the creation of a new dish? It may be the first asparagus in the spring or the gold-fleshed squash of the fall. A moment of contemplation, and the menu is written down. The salad chef goes through the same process, and with a minimum of discussion between the cooks, the salad menu is decided. The baker will discuss the variety and quantities of desserts required for the day, noting any special orders.

With music in the background, the activity has already begun. One morning we listen to Bach, another to the voice of Maria Callas. Some mornings we dance to rock music as pots follow one another on the stove.

The grains for tomorrow's sourdough bread are already simmering, as are the beans for the meal today. Next on the stove, after the soup stock, are the giant soup pot and the boiling water pot, in which vegetables are blanched for the cooked salads.

Some vegetables are peeled, others are just scrubbed. They are diced, sliced thick or thin, cubed, cut into rounds and diagonals, or roughly chopped in preparation for the various dishes. Sea vegetables are soaked, fresh ginger root is grated, garlic is crushed, and lemons are squeezed.

The hand-kneaded and beautifully baked loaves will be out of the oven in time for the first customers who love the warm, hand-sliced bread. Some like it heavily buttered, others prefer the crusty ends.

Beans, grains and vegetables have been transformed into delicious meals to nourish all those who partake of them.

Table of Contents

Appetizers

Soups

Salads

Main Courses

Desserts

Sourdough Bread

October garlic planting

Appetizers

4
Black-eyed Bean Spread

1/2 cup black-eyed beans
2 cups water

Wash beans (they do not need to be soaked). Add water and bring to a boil. Cover and simmer for 45 minutes, or until very soft. In a food processor, grind 2 cloves of garlic (1 teaspoon).

Add:

cooked beans, with cooking liquid
1/8 cup olive oil
1 tbsp umeboshi paste

Process until smooth. Pour into a bowl. Add:

1 finely diced green onion, including green part
1 tbsp chopped fresh dill
1 tbsp finely diced celery
1/4 cup chopped parsley
1 tbsp finely diced carrot
1 tbsp finely diced red and green pepper

Mix with a wooden spoon and refrigerate until cold. Serve with crackers, bread, or vegetable sticks, or use as a sandwich filling.

Yield: 4 to 5 cups

Guacamole

6 small to medium avocadoes
1/4 cup tomato, grated
1/4 cup cucumber, grated
1/4 cup red pepper, finely diced
1/4 cup green pepper, finely diced
1/8 cup onion, grated
1 clove garlic, crushed (about 1/2 tsp)
1/2 tsp ground cumin
pinch of cayenne (as desired)
1/3 cup lemon juice
1 to 1 1/2 tsp salt

Remove peels and pits from avocadoes. Add all other ingredients.
Mash. Taste, adjust lemon and salt.

Yield: 6 cups

garlic flower starburst

Hot Coriander Chutney

1 bunch fresh coriander, finely chopped
2 tbsp umeboshi vinegar
1 - 2 tomatoes, grated
1 small chili pepper, very finely diced *or* 1/2 tsp cayenne

Mix all ingredients in a bowl and serve.

Makes 1 cup

Coriander Chutney

1 large clove garlic
1 fresh chili pepper *or* 1/2 tsp cayenne
1 tsp salt
1 cup coarsely chopped onion
3 cups fresh coriander leaves, washed
1 cup unsweetened dessicated coconut
1/4 lime juice
1 tsp ground cumin
1/2 cup water

In a food processor, grind garlic and chili pepper. Add salt, onion, coconut and water. Grind for 1 minute. Add the rest of the ingredients and process until smooth.

Yield: 2 cups

Hummus

3/4 cup chickpeas
4 cups cold water

Soak chickpeas overnight in cold water. Drain and rinse. Add 4 cups fresh water and pressure cook for 1 hour. If a pressure cooker is not available, bring to a boil and simmer chickpeas for 2 hours, or until soft. Drain cooked chickpeas and reserve cooking liquid.

3 cups cooked chickpeas
3 medium sized cloves fresh garlic
1 tsp ground cumin
3/4 cup chickpea cooking liquid
2 tbsp umeboshi paste
3 tbsp lemon juice
1/4 cup tahini

Place all ingredients in a food processor or blender and blend until very smooth. Cool for 2 - 3 hours. Serve with pita bread, crackers, or vegetable sticks.

Yield: 4 to 5 cups

Raita

2 cups yogourt (goat or cow's milk)
1/2 cup cucumber, diced or in rounds
1 tomato, diced (optional)
1 small onion, diced
1/4 tsp cayenne *or* 1 small hot pepper, finely chopped
1/4 cup chopped fresh coriander or dill

Combine all ingredients. Serve.

Yield: 3 to 4 cups

Pesto

8 medium cloves garlic
1/2 cup pine nuts or walnuts
1 cup parsley leaves
4 cups fresh basil leaves
1/4 cup olive oil
1 1/2 tsp salt

Place all ingredients in a food processor and blend until very smooth.

Yield: 2 cups

Sunset Spread

3 small or medium red peppers, roasted at 400 degrees for 20 to 25 minutes. Remove skins and seeds. Yields about 1/2 cup. Set aside.
1/4 cup arame seaweed, soaked in cold water for 15 minutes, then drained.
1 1/2 cups cream cheese
2 tbsp grated onion
2 tbsp lemon juice
1 tsp salt

Place all ingredients in a food processor and blend until very smooth.

Yield: 3 cups

Tempuna

1 block of tempeh
2 -3 stalks of celery, diced
1/2 red pepper, diced
1/2 red onion, diced
1/3 cup fresh parsley, finely chopped
1 cup soy-based mayonnaise or plain yogourt
1 tbsp dijon mustard
1 - 2 tbsp tamari

Boil tempeh in a pot of water for 15 to 20 minutes. Cool under cold water. Drain. Pat dry.

Crumble tempeh (by hand) into a large mixing bowl. Sprinkle with 1 tbsp tamari. Mix.

In a small bowl, combine mayonnaise or yogourt with mustard.

Add to crumbled tempeh. Stir in chopped vegetables. Add more tamari and/or salt to taste.

Enjoy tempuna as a dip for veggies or corn chips, as a vegetarian alternative to tuna salad, or as a topping for crackers.

10
Sushi

2 cups sushi rice
4 cups water
pinch of salt
8 sheets toasted nori seaweed
1 carrot, cut into thin lengthwise strips and lightly boiled
3 whole green onions, lightly boiled
1 avocado, peeled and thinly sliced
uneboshi vinegar
grated ginger root (optional)

Cook rice until soft. Let cool.

On a sushi mat, place one sheet of nori. Spread a layer of rice (1/4 inch thick or less) to cover 2/3 of the sheet , leaving a bare strip at the top and bottom. In the middle of the rice layer, add filling: 1 slice of carrot, 1 row of sliced avocado, 1/2 green onion. Sprinke with umeboshi vinegar and grated ginger. Roll tightly. Wet edge to seal. Let stand for at least 5 minutes before cutting with a wet knife.

Yield: 8 eight-inch rolls

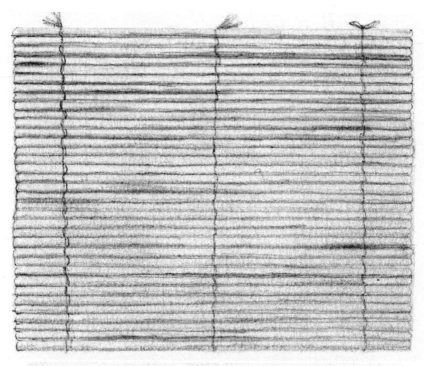

Salsa

1 cup chopped parsley, including stems
2 cloves garlic
1 tsp cumin seed, whole
1 cup onions, coarsely chopped
2 cups tomatoes, halved
1 small hot pepper, seeded
1 sweet red pepper, seeded and roughly chopped
1 green pepper, seeded and roughly chopped
1/2 tsp salt
1/4 cup water
1 bunch chopped fresh coriander

Place all ingredients except coriander in a pot and cook on high heat for 6-10 minutes. Do not overcook. Vegetables should be soft but not mushy. Remove from heat and allow to cool for 30 minutes. Process or blend for a few seconds. Texture should be chunky or smooth as desired. Add fresh coriander to the food processor for the last few seconds.

Pour salsa into a bowl and add:
3 tbsp umeboshi vinegar
3 tbsp lime juice
1/2 tsp cayenne (optional; more if hot salsa is desired)

Makes 3-4 cups

Tofu Spread

1 block (500 g) soft (silken) tofu
2 small cloves garlic
1 tbsp umeboshi paste
1/4 cup almond butter
2 tbsp grated onion or 3 green onions, including green parts, diced
1/2 cup chopped fresh dill or mint

Boil tofu in water to cover for 2 minutes. Drain and cool. In a food processor, mix tofu, garlic, umeboshi paste, almond butter, and onion until well blended and very smooth. Add 1/2 cup fresh dill or mint and process for 1 minute longer. Refrigerate for 2 hours before serving.

Makes 3-4 cups

Soups

Soup Stock

Any vegetable trimmings, such as:
    parsley stems
    carrot ends
    celery leaves
    leek "beards"
1 6-inch piece of kombu seaweed
10-12 cups cold water

In pot, place all vegetable trimmings and kombu; barely cover with cold water. For extra flavour, add bay leaf, thyme, garlic, and a quartered onion. Boil 15 minutes. Strain. The liquid may be used in stews, soups, and vegetable casseroles.

Makes 10 cups

Cream of Asparagus Soup

3 tbsp olive oil
1/2 cup diced onions
1/2 cup diced carrot
1/2 cup diced celery
6 cups asparagus
1/4 cup millet
10 cups soup stock (or water)
1 tsp salt
1/2 cup chopped dill (optional) *or*
1-2 tbsp fresh tarragon or 1 tsp dried tarragon

Trim tough ends of asparagus and use in soup stock Set aside 1 cup of asparagus tips. Slice rest of asparagus into thin pieces.

In soup pot, heat oil and add onion, carrots, celery; cook until soft on medium heat. Add sliced asparagus, soup stock and millet and cook until millet is well done (approximately thirty minutes). Blend soup and return to pot. Add reserved tips and cook 5 minutes longer. Correct salt. Garnish with dill or tarragon and serve.

Serves 6-8

Cream of Celery Soup

3 cups celery, cut into 1/2 inch pieces
1/4 cup millet, washed and drained
6-8 cups soup stock
1 tbsp olive oil
1 cup onion, diced
2 tsp garlic, crushed
1/2 cup carrots, julienne
salt to taste
parsley, chopped, for garnish

In a large pot with a lid, combine celery and millet with 4 1/2 cups soup stock, or water. Cover and bring to a boil. Simmer 20 min, or until celery and millet are cooked.

In another pot, heat oil over medium heat; add onions and sauté until softened. Add garlic and carrots; cook until soft. Add about two cups of more stock; bring to a boil. Reduce heat and simmer.

Transfer celery-millet mixture to a food processor. Purée until very smooth. Add to second pot. Add salt to taste and more stock, or water, if necessary, to achieve desired consistency. Serve garnished with parsley.

Serves 6

Creamy Cauliflower Soup

2 tbsp olive oil
1 cup chopped onion
1 diced leek
1 cup diced carrots
1 cup diced celery
6-8 cups cauliflower (approximately 1 medium sized cauliflower)
1/2 cup millet (washed)
12 cups soup stock
1 teaspoon salt
1/2 cup finely diced parsley

Heat oil and add onions on high heat. Sauté until soft, turn down to medium heat and add leek, carrot and celery. When vegetables are soft, add chopped cauliflower, millet and soup stock; bring to a boil. Turn heat to medium, add salt and simmer for approximately 30-40 minutes until millet is very soft. Blend and serve. Top with diced parsley.

For a creamy soup, blend it all. Otherwise, blend half of the recipe. If too thick, add water.

Serves 10-12

Creamy Corn Soup

3 tbsp olive oil
1/2 cup diced onion
1/2 cup thinly sliced leek, including green leaves
1/2 cup diced carrot
1/2 cup diced celery stalk, including green leaves
2 tsp salt
1/8 tsp cayenne pepper
1 tsp grated fresh ginger
2 cloves garlic, crushed
1 bay leaf
6 cups soup stock
1 cup finely diced fresh tomatoes
1/2 cup diced green pepper
1/2 cup diced red pepper
2 tbsp lime juice
1/4 cup umeboshi vinegar
2 tbsp diced coriander
2 tbsp diced parsley (garnish)
2 cups corn kernels (fresh, off the cob preferred)

In a soup pot, heat olive oil on medium heat. Add onion, leek, carrot, celery and 1/2 tsp of salt. Sauté vegetables until they are soft (about 5-7 minutes). Stir frequently to prevent sticking.

Add cayenne, ginger, garlic, and bay leaf; cook 2 minutes longer. Add soup stock, tomato, corn kernels and remainder of salt; cook 15 minutes. Take half of the soup mixture and process in a food processor or blender, then return it to the pot.

Add red and green pepper, lime juice, umeboshi vinegar. Top with chopped parsley and coriander; serve.

Serves 6-8

Golden Triangle Zucchini Soup

4 to 6 small yellow zucchini
2 cups soup stock (or water if you're in a hurry)
2 tbsp olive oil
1 cup onion, finely diced
2 tsp crushed garlic
2 medium carrots
1/4 tsp ground turmeric
1 yellow sweet pepper
1 inch fresh ginger root, peeled and sliced
3/4 tsp salt, or to taste

Cook 3 or 4 of the zucchinis in the soup stock until very soft. Set
aside. Cut the carrots into triangle shapes: first use the roll cut,
then re-slice each of those pieces.
Heat 1 tbsp olive oil in a soup pot. Add half the onion, then the
garlic. Saute for a minute, stirring; add the carrots and saute gently
for a few more minutes. Meanwhile, blend the cooked zucchini and
the ginger in a food processor until smooth. Add this to the soup
pot.
In a separate pot, gently heat 1 tbsp olive oil, add turmeric,
cook slowly for a minute or two, then add the rest of the onion.
Saute for two minutes; add the sliced pepper and zucchini. A minute
later, add to the soup pot. Use a little of the soup to rinse out this
second pot, thus utilizing all of the flavour and colour.
Add salt, taste and adjust.

yield: 4 to 6

Green Lentil Soup

1 cup green lentils
4 cups water
2 tbsp olive oil
1 diced onion
2 stalks diced celery
1 diced carrot
8 cups water or stock
1 clove garlic, crushed
3 bay leaves
1 tsp salt
1/2 cup chopped parsley

Wash and drain lentils. Add 4 cups water. Bring to a boil on high heat. Lower heat and cook for 5 minutes. Drain. In soup pot, heat oil, sauté onion, carrot and celery until soft. Add water or stock and bring to the boil. Add lentils, garlic, bay leaves and salt. Cook for 20 minutes or until lentils are well cooked. Adjust seasoning if necessary. Serve topped with parsley.

Serves 8-10

Herbed Garlic Soup

6-8 inches wakame seaweed
2 cups cold water
2 tbsp olive oil
1 cup diced onion
10-15 cloves garlic, crushed
10 cups soup stock or water
1 bay leaf
1 tsp dried thyme or 1 sprig fresh thyme
salt to taste
1 bunch chopped parsley
1 bunch green onions, diced

Soak wakame in 2 cups cold water for 10 minutes. Drain, reserving the soaking liquid. Chop wakame finely. In a soup pot heat olive oil on medium heat. Add onions and garlic and sauté 2-3 minutes. Add stock and wakame with soaking liquid. Add bay leaf and thyme and cook for 5 minutes. Salt to taste. Serve topped with parsley and green onions.

Alternatively, tamari or miso may be added in place of salt. If miso is used, add 2-3 tbsp just before serving. Do not cook further after adding miso.

Serves 6-8

Minestrone

3 tbsp olive oil
1 cup diced onions
1 cup diced leeks
1 cup diced carrots
1 cup diced celery
1 cup diced turnip
10 cups of soup stock or water

Heat olive oil in a pot. Add onions and cook until soft. Add leeks, carrots, celery and turnip. Cook until vegetables are soft, about 10 minutes.

Add soup stock. Bring to a boil. Then add:

3 bay leaves
3 cloves garlic, crushed
1/4 cup fresh basil *or* 1 tbsp dried basil
1/2 tsp marjoram
1/2 tsp oregano
1/2 tsp thyme
1 tsp salt
1-2 cups cooked beans (lima, red kidney, pinto, or your choice)
1 cup tomato sauce or juice

Cook soup for 15-20 minutes. Then add:

1 cup diced kale *or* broccoli

Cook 5 minutes longer. When ready, add:

juice of 1-3 lemons
1/2 cup diced parsley.

For a richer soup, add:

1/2 cup of cooked barley *or* 1/2 cup cooked brown rice.

Serves 8-10

Red Lentil and Potato Soup

1 cup red lentils
4 cups water
2 tbsp olive oil
1 cup diced onions
1 tsp ground cumin
2-3 cups potatoes, scrubbed or peeled, and diced
1 1/2 tsp salt
4 cups soup stock or water
1/3 cup lemon juice
1/4 cup chopped fresh coriander

Pick over red lentils to remove dirt or stones. Wash and place in a pot with 4 cups water. Bring to a boil and simmer for 20 minutes. In a soup pot, heat oil on medium heat. Sauté onion and cumin for 5-7 minutes. Stir frequently. Add potatoes and salt, cook for 5 minutes longer. Add lentils (with their cooking liquid). Add soup stock or water. Let cook for 30 minutes on low heat, stirring from time to time. Just before serving, add lemon juice and chopped coriander.

Serves 6-8

Tibetan Bean and Barley Soup

1/2 cup barley, washed and drained
2 cups water

Cook barley in water until soft, about 30 minutes. Do not drain.

2 tbsp olive oil
1/4 tsp of each: ground cumin, turmeric, garam masala, ground cardamom
1 1/2 cups diced onion
1 cup leeks, thinly sliced (1 leek)
2 cloves garlic, crushed
1 cup celery stalks, cut lengthwise then diced
1 cup turnip or rutabaga, diced
1 tsp freshly grated ginger root
1 tsp salt
8 cups soup stock or water
2 bay leaves
2 fresh tomatoes, chopped or grated
1/2 cup tomato sauce (optional)
2 cups cooked beans, any type or a mixture (ie - pinto, black eye, red kidney, lima, navy, mung, chick pea)
1/3 cup lemon juice
1/2 cup chopped fresh coriander
pinch of cayenne (optional)

In a medium-sized soup pot, heat oil, add spices, and roast on low heat until golden. Add onions, leeks, and garlic; cook until soft and wilted (about 5 minutes). Add celery and turnip and cook another 10 minutes. Add grated ginger root and salt. Add stock or water, bay leaf, grated tomatoes and bring to a boil. Add barley (with cooking liquid) and beans; simmer 30 minutes. Stir in lemon juice and coriander just before serving.

Serves 8-10

Squash Soup

5 cups buttercup, red kuri, or other winter squash, washed, seeded and cubed
8 cups of water

Cook squash in water until tender, approximately 30 minutes. Do not drain.

2 tbsp olive oil
1 large diced onion
1 diced celery stalk
1 large diced carrot
1 leek, sliced
1 tsp freshly grated ginger root
2 cloves garlic
pinch of cayenne (optional)
salt
2 bay leaves

Heat olive oil in soup pot on medium high heat. Add onions and cook until transparent. Add celery, carrot, leek, ginger, garlic and cayenne. Add 1-2 cups liquid from cooked squash. Cook on low heat until vegetables are soft: 20-30 minutes. Add salt to taste.

In a blender, blend the cooked squash with remaining liquid and combine with soup in pot. Add bay leaves. Adjust seasoning. Bring to a boil again on low heat. Serve.

Serves 8-10

Yellow Split Pea Soup

1 cup yellow split peas
4 cups of water

Wash peas well and drain. In a pot, place peas and cover with water. Bring to a boil on high heat. Lower heat and simmer for 30-45 minutes, covered.

2 tbsp olive oil
1 cup finely diced onion
1 cup finely diced carrot
1-2 cups finely diced leek
1 cup finely diced celery stalk
1 cup finely diced rutabaga
6 cups soup stock or water
1-2 tsp of salt, or to taste
2 bay leaves
1/2 cup finely chopped parsley

In a soup pot, heat olive oil. Add diced onion, carrot, leek, celery, and rutabaga and gently sauté until soft. Add soup stock and bring to a boil. Add cooked split peas (with cooking liquid), pinch of salt, and bay leaves. Reduce to simmer and cook for 30 minutes, stirring occasionally. If necessary, place heat diffuser under pot to minimize sticking. Serve topped with freshly chopped parsley.

Serves 10-12

Zucchini Soup

1 kg small green zucchini (5 cups)
1 clove garlic
1 tsp salt
8   cups stock or water
2 tbsp olive oil
1 onion, diced
1 carrot, diced
1/2 cup chopped parsley *or* dill

Dice one zucchini into small cubes; set aside. Boil remaining zucchini, garlic and salt in water or stock until zucchini is soft.

In a soup pot heat oil. Add onion and carrot, and cook until wilted. Add diced zucchini.

Blend cooked zucchini and soup stock and add to soup pot. Correct seasoning. Serve topped with parsley or dill.

Serves 8-10

Salads

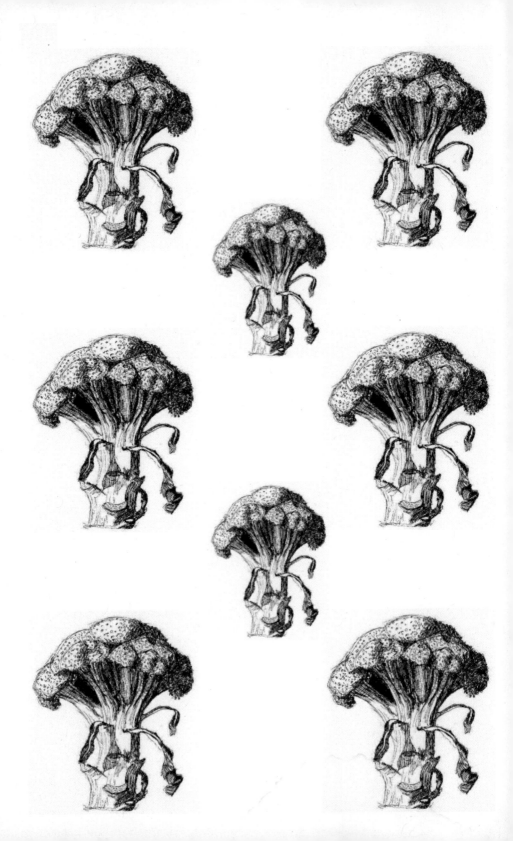

Broccoli Salad

1-2 bunches broccoli
4-6 litres water

Boil water in pot, cut broccoli into florets, peel and slice stems.

For best results, blanch broccoli in small batches by dropping a hand-ful at a time into boiling water. Lift out with a slotted spoon within 2-3 minutes. Do not overcook. Cool quickly in ice water to retain dark green colour. Drain.

1/2 red pepper, sliced
1/2 green pepper, sliced
3 green onions, diced
1 cup chopped parsley
1/2 carrot, sliced on the diagonal
1 small celery stalk, sliced on the diagonal
1/2 cup finely chopped fresh basil *or* 1 tbsp rubbed dried basil
3 - 4 tbsp olive oil
1/2 - 1 tsp salt

In a large bowl mix all salad ingredients.

Serves 6-8

Carrot Salad

4   tbsp lemon juice
6 tbsp orange juice
2 tsp juice of freshly grated ginger root
6 cups grated carrots

Mix lemon and orange juice, and add ginger juice. Pour over grated carrots and mix well.

Serves 8 - 10

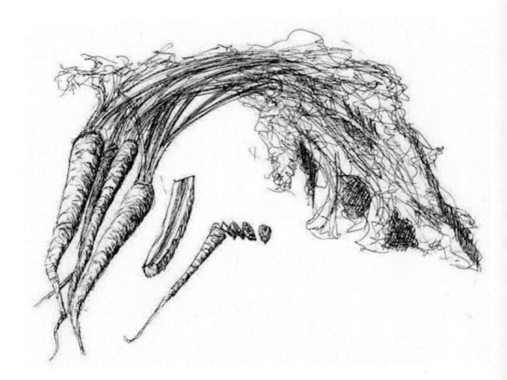

Caesar Salad

1 Romaine lettuce washed and torn into bite sized pieces.

Dressing
1/2 block soft tofu (250 g)
1 tsp umeboshi paste
1-2 lemons, juice only
1 tsp prepared yellow mustard
1 tbsp olive oil
2 cloves garlic
1/2 cup water
1/2 tsp salt

Blend all dressing ingredients until creamy and smooth.

Place lettuce in a bowl. Add dressing and toss.

Serves 8-10

Clear Noodle Salad (Mung Bean Thread Noodles)

Burdock
2 cups burdock root, scraped or scrubbed, cut in thin diagonal slices
8-10 cups water

Boil water and add sliced burdock. Cook for 5 minutes. Drain and
set aside. Reserve boiling water.

Noodles
mung bean thread noodles (225 g)
burdock broth

Add noodles to boiling broth, turn off heat and let sit for 10 minutes.
Drain and cool.

Seaweed
1/2 cup dry hiziki seaweed
2 cups water

Soak hiziki for 1 hour in 2 cups water. Drain and squeeze out excess
liquid. Set aside.

Vegetables
1 cup carrot, cut in thin diagonal slices
1 cup sliced celery
1/2 red pepper, sliced
1/2 green pepper, sliced
2 cups finely chopped parsley
1 cup green onions, thinly sliced on diagonal, including green parts
1/2 English cucumber, thinly sliced

Prepare the vegetables and place in a large bowl. Add drained burdock, hiziki, and noodles.

Dressing
1 tbsp garlic, crushed
1 tbsp ginger, grated
1/2 cup tamari
1/4 cup dark sesame oil
1/4 - 1/2 cup fresh lemon juice or brown rice vinegar

Pour dressing over mixture, mix and serve.

Serves 8-10

Corn Hiziki Salad

1/2 cup dry hiziki seaweed
2 cups water

Soak hiziki in water for 1 hour. Drain and discard soaking liquid. Set aside.

3 cups corn kernels
2 cups chopped parsley
1 red pepper, diced
1 green pepper, diced
1 English cucumber, thinly sliced
1 bunch green onions, thin diagonal slices
1 carrot, thin diagonal slices

In a large bowl, mix drained hiziki, corn, parsley, red and green pepper, cucumber, onions, and carrots.

Dressing
2 cloves garlic, crushed
2 tsp ginger, grated
1/4 cup tamari
1/4 cup brown rice vinegar
1/4 cup dark sesame oil

Pour dressing over salad and mix well. Serve.

For a more substantial salad, 1-2 cups of cooked noodles such as shells or spirals may be added to vegetables before dressing. In this case the dressing may need more tamari and/or rice vinegar.

Soaking liquid from hiziki may be used to water indoor plants.

Serves 8-10

Fiddlehead, Burdock, Carrot Salad

1 cup burdock (1 root), scrubbed and thinly sliced on the diagonal
2 litres water

Bring water to boil. Add burdock. Simmer for 5 min. Drain and cool. Set aside.

In same water, add:

2 cups fiddleheads

Cook for 2 minutes. Drain and cool. Set aside.

1/4 cup dry hiziki sea vegetable
2 cups water

Soak hiziki in water for 1 hour. Strain and squeeze out excess liquid. Set aside.

1/2 red pepper, diced
1 cup carrots, scrubbed, and sliced on the diagonal
3 thinly sliced green onions, including the green part
1 cup chopped parsley

Dressing
1/4 cup tamari soy-sauce
1/8 cup rice vinegar
2 tbsp dark sesame oil
1 tsp ginger root, grated (measure after grating)
1 clove garlic, crushed

Combine all salad ingredients, pour dressing over them, mix well and serve.

Burdock broth makes a delicious stock for soups or for cooking pasta; it also makes a strengthening, blood-cleansing drink.

Serves 6-8

Fresh Seaweed Salad

1 cup fresh wakame seaweed

Fresh seaweed is available at some Asian markets. As it is shipped salt-packed, it is necessary to rinse the seaweed in a colander under cold running water for a few minutes to remove the salt. Then, soak in 2 cups of filtered or spring water for 1/2 hour. Drain. Squeeze out excess moisture. Chop. Mix with:

1/4 cup parsley, chopped
1/4 cup green onions, chopped

Set aside.

Dressing
1/2 tsp mirin
2 tbsp lemon juice
1 tbsp dark sesame oil
2 tbsp sweet brown rice vinegar
4 tbsp tamari
1 tsp fresh ginger, grated
1 clove garlic, crushed

Line a salad bowl with lettuce leaves. Dress seaweed. Fill salad bowl. Serve topped with a sprinkle of finely diced red pepper.

Serves 6

Garlic Beets

5-6 medium sized beets
2-3 tbsp olive oil
1-2 cloves garlic
2 tbsp umeboshi vinegar

Place beets in a pot, cover with water and bring to a rolling boil on high heat. Reduce heat, cover pot and simmer until beets are tender. Cooking time will depend on the size and age of the beets. Freshly dug small beets will cook faster than stored or large ones.

Peel the beets while still warm and allow to cool completely. Slice or chop the beets or serve whole. Place in bowl.
Separately, crush the garlic and mix with the oil and umeboshi vinegar. Pour over beets, mix and serve.

Serves 8-10

Greek Salad

3 ripe tomatoes, sliced
1 red pepper, seeded, washed and sliced
1 green pepper, seeded, washed and sliced
1 medium onion, sliced
1 English cucumber, sliced
1 cup goat's milk feta cheese, cut into small cubes
1/2 cup black olives, rinsed

Dressing
1 clove garlic, crushed
1/2 tsp dried rubbed basil
1/2 cup olive oil
1/3 cup umeboshi plum vinegar
1/2 cup chopped parsley

In a large bowl slice tomatoes, peppers (green and red), onion, and cucumber. Add feta cheese, olives and mix gently. Pour vinegar, garlic, basil, and half of the parsley over vegetables and mix again. Place salad in serving bowl and sprinkle remaining parsley over top.

Serves 8-10

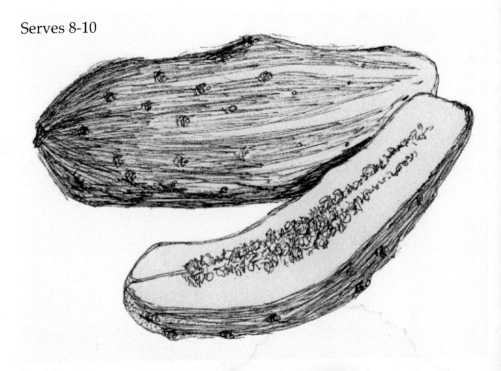

Green Bean Salad

1 1/2 lbs green beans
1 carrot thinly sliced, diagonally
1 celery stalk sliced, diagonally
1/2 red pepper, diced in large pieces
1/2 green pepper, diced in large pieces
1 cup finely chopped parsley,
2 tbsp dried rubbed basil *or* 1/2 cup finely chopped fresh basil
1/2 cup thinly sliced purple cabbage
1/4 cup olive oil
1/2 tsp salt, or to taste

Remove stem end but leave green bean whole. In a large pot, boil 3 litres of water. Blanch beans by dropping small batches into a pot of boiling water for 2 minutes. Drain and cool quickly to retain dark green colour.

Mix all ingredients in large bowl and serve.

Serves 8 - 10

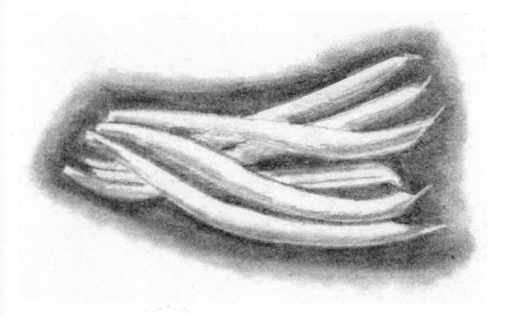

Green Salad With Ginger Garlic Dressing

10 cups mixed salad greens (Romaine, red leaf, watercress, radichio, spinach, dandelion, or any other)
1 small cucumber, cut into thin round slices
1 red pepper, cut into thin slices
1 green pepper, cut into thin slices
2 celery stalks, cut into thin diagonal slices
1 large carrot, cut into thin half-moon slices
1/2 small red cabbage, cored and thinly sliced (2 cups)

Break greens into bite size pieces using fingers - never use a knife to cut salad greens! Add suggested assortment of vegetables to green leaves; experiment with your own combinations! Mix leaves and vegetables together.

Dressing
1/4 cup dark sesame oil
1/8 cup fresh lemon juice
1/8 cup sweet brown rice vinegar
1/8 cup tamari, or to taste
2 small cloves crushed garlic
1 tsp freshly grated ginger root

Combine all ingredients in jar. Shake well just before dressing salad. Pour over greens and toss.

Serves 8 - 10

Green Salad with Lemon Vinaigrette

Mixed salad greens, such as:

leaf lettuce
Romaine lettuce
Boston lettuce
spinach leaves
watercress
arugala
mache
radichio
or any other

1 English cucumber, thinly sliced.
1-2 carrots, shredded or sliced
1 bunch green onions diced (optional)
1 red pepper, diced

Wash and drain salad greens. Shred the greens into a bowl with other ingredients. Toss.

Lemon Vinaigrette
1/2 cup lemon juice, freshly squeezed
1/2 cup olive oil
2 cloves garlic, crushed
2 tbsp finely chopped fresh basil *or* 1 tsp dried rubbed basil
1 tsp salt

Combine dressing ingredients, pour over salad and toss well.

Vinaigrette can be made in small or large quantities as needed. Mix dressing in a jar and refrigerate unused portion.

Serves 8-10

Japanese Noodle Salad

Burdock and Noodles
12 cups of water
1-2 cups burdock, scrubbed and thinly sliced on the diagonal

500 g rice, buckwheat, or wheat noodles

Bring water to a boil. Add burdock and boil for 3 minutes. Remove burdock and set aside. In the same water, boil noodles and cook according to directions on package. Drain and cool.

Vegetables
1 cup diced carrot
1 cup diced celery
1 1/2 cups diced green onions
1 cup chopped purple cabbage
1 cup chopped red pepper
1 cup chopped green pepper
1/2 cup hiziki seaweed, soaked in 2 cups water for 1 hour and drained

Combine vegetables and set aside.

Dressing
1 tbsp garlic, crushed
3 tbsp ginger root, grated
2 tbsp dark sesame oil
4 tbsp tamari
3 tbsp umeboshi vinegar
1 tsp mirin

Combine dressing ingredients.

In a large bowl, combine vegetables, noodles, burdock and seaweed.

Combine dressing and pour over salad. Mix again and serve.

Serves 10-12

Land and Sea Salad

1 litre water
1 burdock root, thin diagonal slices
1 lotus root, thin diagonal slices
1 carrot, thin diagonal slices
1/4 cup hiziki seaweed
2 cups cold water
1/2 cup parsley, diced
1 bunch green onions, including green part, diced

In a pot, bring the litre of water to a boil. Add burdock root, simmer for 5 minutes. Remove burdock, cool, and set aside. In the same water, simmer carrot for 2 minutes; remove, cool, and set aside. For treatment of lotus root, refer to page 51. Soak hiziki in the cup of cold water for one hour. Drain, set aside.

Dressing
2 tbsp sweet brown rice vinegar
2 tbsp lemon juice
1/2 tsp mirin
1 tbsp tamari
1 tbsp dark sesame oil
1/2 tsp salt
1 tsp fresh ginger root, grated

Combine burdock, lotus root, carrot, and hiziki. Pour dressing over vegetables. Mix. Garnish with parsley and green onions. Can be served over mesclun salad mix or fresh spinach leaves.

Serves 6

Lima Bean Salad

1 cup lima beans
4 cups water

Wash and soak beans in water for 4-12 hours. Drain.

4 cups water
1 piece kombu, 2 inches long

Place beans and kombu in pot with 4 cups fresh water. Bring to a boil. Cover and cook on minimum heat until beans are soft, not mushy. Drain and reserve the cooking liquid. Place beans in the refrigerator to cool.

1 cup chopped parsley
1 cup chopped fresh basil *or* 1/4 cup dried rubbed basil
2 cloves garlic
2 tbsp lemon juice
1 tbsp umeboshi paste
2 tbsp olive oil
1/2 cup cooking liquid from beans
1/2 cup lima beans

Place parsley, basil, garlic, lemon juice, umeboshi paste, olive oil, and 1/2 cup cooking liquid from beans in blender. Blend lightly. Add 1/2 cup lima beans and blend to make a creamy green dressing.

Place cooked lima beans in a large bowl. Add dressing and mix well. Serve with whole lettuce leaves.

Serves 6

Lotus Root Salad

1 or 2 lotus roots, about 500 g

Peel the lotus roots; slice thinly into rounds. Colour should be whitish throughout. Grey or brown inside indicates the presence of molds.

Bring two litres of water to a boil. Add sliced lotus root. Reduce heat to a minimum to prevent boiling. Allow the lotus root to sit in the water for five minutes. Drain and cool.

Dressing

1/4 cup sweet brown rice vinegar
1/4 cup lemon juice
1/2 tsp fresh ginger root, grated
1/2 tsp salt
1 tsp mirin

Place dressing in a jar. Add drained, cooled lotus root. Will keep under refrigeration for two weeks. To serve, place 4 or 5 slices per person in a small bowl. Garnish with thin slivers of nori seaweed.

Marinated Mushrooms

10 cups small white mushrooms, washed

Place 5 cups of water in a pot and bring to a boil. Add mushrooms. Return to a boil. Cook for 1 minute, drain and cool.

Dressing
1/4 cup olive oil
1/4 cup umeboshi vinegar
2 cloves garlic crushed
1 tsp dried rubbed basil

Place mushrooms in a bowl; add dressing and mix well.

Serves 10

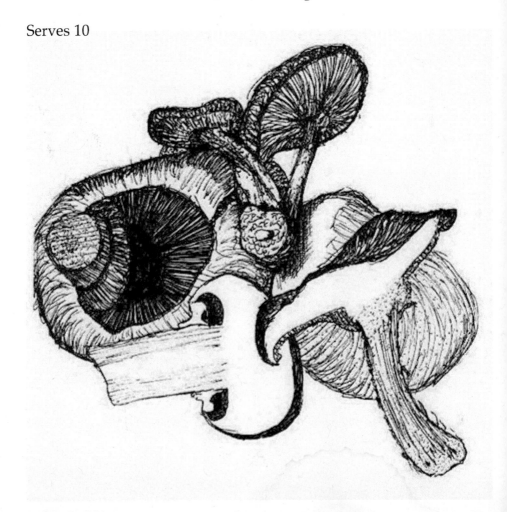

Oriental Nappa Cabbage Salad

Vegetables
6 cups nappa cabbage, thinly sliced
1 carrot, diagonally sliced
1 bunch green onions, diagonally sliced
1 red pepper, seeded, thinly sliced
1 green pepper, seeded, thinly sliced
1 cup finely chopped parsley
1/2 - 1 cup finely chopped fresh coriander

Blanch sliced nappa in boiling water for two minutes. Drain and cool. In a large bowl, mix all vegetables and pour dressing over them. Mix and serve.

Dressing
1/2 cup tamari
1/2 cup lemon juice
2 tsp grated ginger root
2 tsp crushed garlic
1/4 cup dark sesame oil
1/4 to 1/2 tsp cayenne or whole, finely chopped hot pepper

Serves 8-10

Orzo Salad

2 cups uncooked orzo
4 to 5 sundried tomatoes (finely sliced)
1 cup thinly sliced eggplant (optional)
1/2 cup thinly sliced zucchini (optional)
1 cup finely chopped red peppers (optional)
3 tbsp olive oil for vegetables
3 tbsp olive oil for salad
1 tsp salt for vegetables
1 tsp salt for salad
1/4 cup feta cheese, crumbled
1/4 cup olives
1/4 cup fresh parsley, finely chopped
1 tbsp dried basil
1 tbsp lemon juice

Cook orzo in a large pot of boiling water according to package instructions. Meanwhile, in separate bowls, toss eggplant, zucchini. and red peppers with a small amount of olive oil and salt. Roast in a 350 degree oven until lightly browned. The zucchini and red pepper will roast more quickly than the aubergine.

Once the orzo is cooked, cool under cold water. Drain. Toss with remaining olive oil. Add sundried tomatoes, feta cheese, olives, lemon juice, basil, parsley and salt. Carefully stir in cooled roasted vegetables. Add more salt and lemon juice to taste.

Serves 6

Parsnip Salad with Japanese Dressing

Parsnips, use about 2 1/2 pounds. Best when dug in the spring.
Cut into chunks; the roll cut works well. This will result
in a basically three-sided form, though one of the sides is
curved. As you are cutting each parsnip, pay attention to
achieve a close to equal volume with each cut piece.
Therefore, the pieces cut from the narrow end of the parsnip
will be longer than those at the wide-shouldered top end.
Often, a parsnip will have extremely broad shoulders (and
a narrow waist!); cut the wider part lengthwise prior to
finally finishingwith its three-sided form.
Toss with olive oil. Lightly salt. Spread on baking pan lined
with parchment paper. Bake at 350 degrees until tender
(about 40 to 50 minutes).

Dressing:
1 tbsp grated ginger
1 tbsp crushed garlic
2 tbsp tamari
1/2 tbsp dark sesame oil
1 tbsp rice vinegar
1 tbsp mirin
the juice of 1 lemon

Garnish:
Arame seaweed (soaked for 20 minutes and drained), green onion,
sliced, red pepper, diced, and finely chopped parsley.

Quinoa Tabouleh

Grain
1 cup quinoa grain
1 1/2 tsp sea salt
1 3/4 cups water

Wash and drain quinoa. Place quinoa, water, and salt in a pot and bring to a boil on medium-high heat. Cover pan and turn heat down to simmer for 20-25 minutes. Cool.

Vegetables
2 cups finely chopped parsley
1 cup green onions, finely diced, including green part
1 small carrot, diced finely (1 cup)
1/2 red pepper, diced (1/2 cup)
1/2 green pepper, diced (1/2 cup)
1/2 cup fresh mint leaves, chopped very finely
or 3 tbsp dried rubbed mint leaves

Dressing
1/3 –1/2 cup extra virgin olive oil
1/4 cup lemon juice
2 garlic cloves, crushed

Add vegetables and dressing to bowl of quinoa and mix well. Line a platter with lettuce leaves, place salad on leaves and garnish with thin slices of lemon and black olives.

Serves 8-10

See page 104 for information on quinoa.

Roasted Red Pepper Dressing

1 red pepper
1 tomato
1/2 cup water
1/4 cup olive oil
2 tbsp lemon juice
1 tbsp dried basil
1 tsp salt
1 tbsp umeboshi vinegar
1 tbsp garlic

Cut red pepper in half, discard seeds and membranes. Toss with a small amount of salt and oil. Roast in 350 degree oven until soft. Cool. Place pepper and all other ingredients in blender. Blend until smooth.

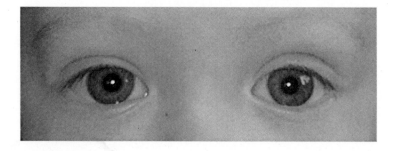

Raw Onion Salad

2 Spanish onions, diced very finely (4 cups)
1-2 tbsp umeboshi vinegar
1/4 cup freshly chopped coriander
1 small chili pepper, very finely diced, or 1/4 tsp cayenne

Marinate onions in vinegar 15-20 minutes. Add remaining ingredients, mix well and serve.

Spoon over curries, beans or grains. Will keep, refrigerated, for one week.

Makes 15-20 small servings

Roasted Eggplant Salad

3 large *or* 6 small eggplants
1 tsp salt

Wash eggplants and remove green stems. Slice into rounds 1/3 inch thick. In a large bowl toss eggplant with salt. Place slices onto cookie sheet and bake for 30 - 45 minutes or until eggplant is dry and light brown. Let cool.

In a bowl, place:

1 Spanish or red onion, thinly sliced (2 cups)
2 tbsp umeboshi vinegar

Marinate for 20 min. Add:

2 tomatoes, cut into wedges
2 cloves garlic, crushed
1 tsp roasted and freshly ground cumin
juice of 1-2 lemons (1/4 cup)
1/3 cup olive oil
1 cup chopped parsley
1 green pepper, thinly sliced

Combine cooked eggplant with rest of ingredients. Mix well. Adjust salt or lemon if necessary.

Serves 6-8

Rye Berry Salad

Grain
1 cup rye berries
4 cups water

Wash rye berries and soak overnight in water. Drain and rinse. Add 3 cups of cold water. Bring to a boil on high heat. Cover and simmer for 30 minutes. drain and cool.

Vegetables
1 bunch green onions, diced, including green parts
1 cup chopped parsley
1/2 cup chopped fresh dill
1/2 cup finely diced carrots
1/4 cup finely diced red pepper
1/4 cup finely diced green pepper

Mix diced vegetables with cooled grain.

Dressing
1/2 cup lemon juice
1/4 cup olive oil
1/2 tsp salt, or to taste

Mix dressing. Pour over grain and vegetables, adjust salt or lemon if necessary, and serve.

Serves 6-8

Squash Salad

4 cups butternut squash, scrubbed, seeded and cubed
1/2 tsp salt
1 tbsp olive oil
In a large bowl, toss the cubed squash with salt and oil. Spread in a
single layer upon a parchment paper lined cookie sheet. Roast at
350 degrees for about 30 minutes, or until just soft but not mushy.
Allow to cool.

1/2 cup burdock root, scrubbed and sliced into thin diagonals
2 to 3 cups water
Drop the sliced burdock root into boiling water. Cook for 5 minutes.
Drain and cool.

1/4 cup hiziki or arame seaweed
2 cups water
Soak the seaweed in 2 cups of water until soft (30 to 60 minutes).
Drain and squeeze out excess moisture.

1/2 cup thinly sliced green onion, including green parts
1 cup chopped parsley
Mix together the cooled squash and burdock root with the drained
hiziki, green onions, and parsley.

Dressing
1 tsp fresh ginger root, grated
1/2 tsp garlic, crushed
1/4 cup dark sesame oil
1/3 cup tamari
1/3 cup freshly squeezed lemon juice
Mix dressing ingredients.
Pour over salad and toss.

Serves 8

Thai Noodle Salad

Burdock
2 cups burdock root, scraped or scrubbed, sliced into thin diagonals
8-10 cups water

Boil water and add sliced burdock. Cook for 5 minutes. Drain and set aside. Reserve cooking liquid.

Noodles
225 g buckwheat or udon or rice noodles

Cook noodles in burdock broth. Drain and cool. Set aside.

Seaweed
1/2 cup dry hiziki or arame seaweed

Soak seaweed in 2 cups of water for 30 to 60 minutes. Drain.
Squeeze out excess liquid. Set aside.

Vegetables
1 stalk celery, thin diagonal slices
1 medium carrot, thin diagonal slices
1 bunch green onions, thin diagonal slices
1 large red pepper, diced
1 large green pepper, diced
2 cups parsley, finely chopped
1/2 cup red cabbage, thinly sliced

Combine all salad ingredients in large bowl.

Dressing
1 cup peanut butter (smooth)
1/2 cup tamari
1/2 cup lime juice
2 tsp ginger, grated
2 tsp garlic, crushed
1/2-1 cup water
1/4 tsp cayenne

Blend or process dressing ingredients until smooth. Mix with salad ingredients.

Serves 10-12

Tofu Salad

Mix together the following marinade:

1/4 cup tamari
1 cup water
2 cloves garlic, crushed
2 tsp ginger, grated
1 block firm tofu (400-500 g), cut into slices 3/4 inch thick.

Marinate six to eight hours.

Meanwhile:

1/4 cup hiziki seaweed

Soak in 1 cup water for one hour. Drain. Squeeze out excess liquid. Remove tofu from marinade. Place slices on parchment paper, on a cookie sheet. Bake at 350° F for one hour, or an hour and a quarter, until brown. Cool. Cut each slice into quarters:

To the cooled sliced tofu, add:

1/2 cup parsley, diced
1/2 cup green onions, including the green part, thinly sliced
1/4 cup red pepper, diced
1/4 cup green pepper, diced
1/4 cup carrot, thinly sliced
1/4 cup celery, thinly sliced
the previously soaked hiziki

Dressing
1 large clove garlic, crushed
3 tbsp lemon juice
1 tbsp dark sesame oil
1 tbsp sweet brown rice vinegar
1/2 tsp mirin
3 tbsp tamari
1 tsp grated ginger

Mix dressing. Pour over tofu and vegetables. Mix well.

Serves 6

Variation: add 2 tbsp prepared yellow mustard to the dressing.

Main Courses

Angelica Casserole

Grain
1 cup millet
2 1/2 cups water
1/2 tsp salt

Wash millet well. Drain. Add 2 1/2 cups water and salt. Bring to a boil on high heat. Reduce heat to minimum, cover and cook until soft: 20 to 30 minutes. Set aside.

Vegetables
4 cups cauliflower (about one small sized one)
3 cups water

Wash and cut cauliflower. Boil water in pot. Add cauliflower and cook until soft, 20 to 25 minutes. Drain, reserving cooking liquid.

1 cup almonds

Grind almonds in a food processor until fine (breadcrumb consistency).

2 tbsp umeboshi paste

In a pot or bowl, place cooked millet, cooked cauliflower, ground almonds and umeboshi paste. Add 1/2 to 1 cup of the cauliflower cooking liquid. Mash until smooth. Place mixture in a casserole dish. Bake at 350 degrees for 15 minutes, covered.

Topping
1/2 cup water
1/4 cup finely diced leeks
1/4 cup finely diced squash
1/4 cup finely diced turnip
1/4 cup finely diced carrot
2 tsp grated ginger root
2 to 3 tbsp tamari
2 tbsp arowroot dissolved in 1/4 cup cold water

Bring water to a boil. Add leeks, squash, turnip and carrot. Add ginger and tamari. Cook until vegetables are tender, only a couple of minutes. Add water/arrowroot mixture, and stir until thickened. Remove from heat. Spoon over millet-cauliflower-almond.

Serves 8 to 10.

Aduki Beans

1 cup aduki beans
4 cups water
6 inch piece of kombu sea vegetable (optional)

Wash beans and soak in water for 6 to 8 hours or overnight. Drain and discard soaking water. Add 4 cups fresh water and bring to a boil. Reduce heat and simmer for 45-60 minutes until beans are soft.

Aduki beans can be served with baked squash (see p 70).

Serves 6-8

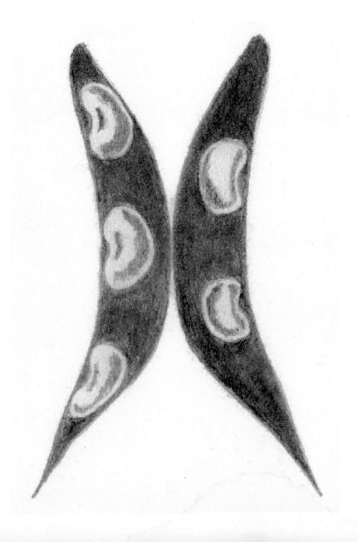

Arame

1 cup arame (dry measure)
water to cover
2 tsp dark sesame oil
2 small or 1 large onion, cut into large chunks
2 tsp grated ginger root
2 cloves garlic, crushed
1 cup water
1/8 - 1/4 cup tamari
1 tablespoon umeboshi vinegar

Soak arame in water for 15 minutes. Drain.

Heat oil and sauté the onion. When onion begins to brown, add the ginger, garlic and 1 cup water. When this mixture is boiling, add the drained arame, return to the boil and cook for 2 minutes. Add tamari and umeboshi and serve.

Serves 8-12

Baked Squash

1 medium buttercup or butternut squash (1 1/2 kg)
olive oil for coating (1 tbsp)
1/2 tsp salt

Wash squash under cold running water, scrubbing skin with vegetable brush. Halve and scoop out seeds and fibres.

If using butternut squash, cut horizontally into 1/2 inch rounds. Place squash in bowl, coat lightly with oil and salt. Place on baking sheet and roast at 350°F for 25-30 minutes, or until golden and soft.

For buttercup squash, seed and cut into 1 inch cubes and proceed as above. Cooking time is generally the same, although this will depend on size of cubes.

Serves 8-10

Black Soybeans

1 cup black soybeans
4 inch piece of kombu seaweed
1 tbsp dark sesame oil
1 burdock root, sliced (approximately 1/2 cup)
1 cup diced onion
1 cup diced carrot
tamari

Wash soybeans and soak in 8 cups of water for 6-12 hours or over-night. Drain. Add 4 cups of water and kombu. Bring to a boil, cover, reduce heat and simmer for 1 hour. Do not drain.

Heat oil in pot. Sauté onions in oil, then add burdock root and carrot. When vegetables are partially cooked, add beans. Simmer until beans are done: 1-1 1/2 hours. Add tamari to taste.

Serves 6

Black-eyed Beans with Fennel

1 cup black-eyed beans, washed
4 cups water

It is not necessary to soak black-eyed beans. Place washed beans in pot, add water and bring to a boil on high heat. Reduce heat to minimum and cook for 15 minutes. Drain and put aside.

3 tbsp olive oil
1/2 cup diced onion
1 cup diced tomatoes (optional)
1 fresh fennel root, including green leaves, diced
4-5 cloves garlic, crushed
salt to taste
1-2 cups water

Heat olive oil in a pot and add onions. Cook until soft and add carrots. Cook 5 minutes. Add drained beans, tomatoes, garlic, fennel, salt, and water. Simmer covered until beans are soft but not mushy: 20-30 minutes.

Serves 6-8

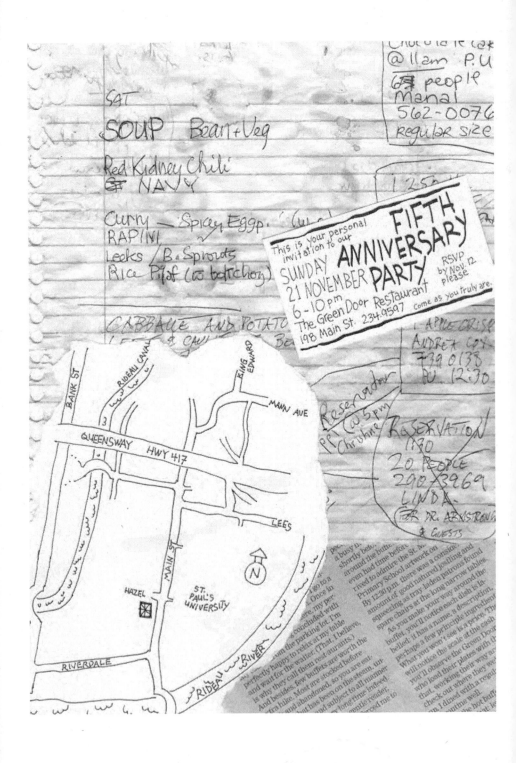

Brown Rice

1 cup short or long grain organic brown rice
2 cups water
1/2 tsp salt

Wash rice and drain. Place rice, water and salt in a pot. Bring to the boil on high heat, uncovered. Reduce heat to minimum, cover, and simmer until cooked, approximately 45-60 minutes.

Variations:

Substitute part or half the brown rice for an equal amount of wild rice, wehani, or basmati. Use same method.

Serves 4-6

Buckwheat Noodles with Ginger Garlic Sauce

3 litres (12 cups) water
225 g buckwheat, udon, or rice noodles

In large size pot, bring water to a boil. Add noodles and cook 5 - 7 minutes, or until cooked. Do not overcook. Stir once or twice during cooking to prevent sticking. Drain.

Sauce
2 tsp fresh ginger, grated
2 tsp garlic, crushed
4 tbsp olive oil
5 tbsp tamari soy sauce

Mix all sauce ingredients into a bowl big enough to hold noodles. Add drained noodles to sauce and mix.

Serves 8-10

Cabbage Rolls

1 1/2 cups diced onion
2 cups basmati or arborio rice
1 1/2 cups chopped parsley
1 1/2 cups chopped dill
1 cup chopped fesh mint leaves *or* 3 tbsp dried rubbed mint leaves
2 tsp salt
2 cloves garlic, crushed
1/2-3/4 cups olive oil
1 cup water *or* 1/2 cup of tomato sauce and 1/2 cup water

Blanch 24-30 cabbage leaves in boiling water for 2 minutes. Drain and cool.

Wash and drain rice

In a bowl, mix onions, rice, parsley, dill, mint, salt, garlic, and oil. Mix very well, preferably with hands, adding 1 cup of water, or 1/2 cup tomato sauce and 1/2 cup water.

Place 1-2 tbsp of mixture in each leaf according to the size of the leaf. Fold in the sides and roll tightly to form a roll. Place in pan, seam side down and close together. Layer rolls in pan and continue until filling and leaves are all used. Very gently, pour enough water (or water and tomato sauce) to just cover the rolls.

Place a fireproof plate snugly over the rolls inside the pot to weigh down the leaves. Cover. Bring to a boil, then reduce heat to minimum and simmer for 30-40 minutes until done. You may add the juice of 1-2 lemons before serving.

Makes 24-30 rolls

Cauliflower and Potato Curry

4 tbsp olive oil *or* 2 tbsp olive oil and 2 tbsp butter
1/4 tsp each: asafoetida, cardamom, cayenne
1/2 tsp each: ground turmeric, cumin
1 tsp each garam masala and ground coriander
3 cloves garlic
1 small head cauliflower, cut into florets
1 1/2 pounds potato, scrubbed and cut into medium size chunks
1-2 cups water
salt to taste
2 cups (500 ml) coconut milk, unsweetened*
1/2 each: red and green pepper, diced
1 cup fresh, diced tomato
1/2 cup chopped fresh coriander

In a medium size pot, bring oil and butter to medium-low heat. Add spices and toast lightly. Add garlic, cauliflower and potato and sauté for 5 minutes on medium heat. Add water, salt and coconut and cook until potato is soft when punctured with a fork. Add peppers, tomato and coriander and cook another 5 minutes. Adjust seasoning and serve.

* Choose a variety of coconut milk that contains no preservatives.

Serves 6-8

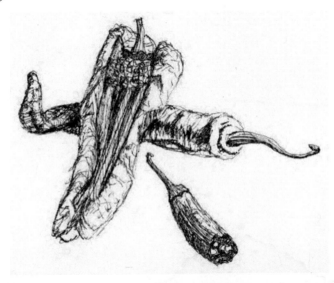

Chick Peas In Lemon Sauce

1 cup dried chick peas
4 cups water

Sort chick peas, discarding any stones and dirt. Wash and soak in water overnight. Drain. Add 4 cups water to a pot with the chick peas and bring to boil on high heat. Reduce heat to minimum and simmer until chick peas are soft – up to 2 hours.

Alternatively, pressure cook soaked chick peas for 45-60 minutes.

1 tbsp olive oil
1 cup diced onion
1 tsp salt
2-3 lemons, juice only
1-2 tbsp arrowroot

Heat oil in a separate pot and add onions and salt. Cook until soft. Add the chick peas and enough of their cooking liquid to just cover. Simmer until chick peas are well done.

Dissolve arrowroot in lemon juice and add to pot, stirring until slightly thickened.

Adjust salt. Serve.

Serves 6-8

Chickpea and Wild Rice Vegetable Pie

Filling
3/4 cup chickpeas
4 cups cold water
or 2 cups cooked chick peas (to cook chickpeas, see p 79); drain,
 reserving cooking liquid.

1/2 cup wild rice
1 cup water
1/2 tsp salt
Wash rice and drain. Place rice, water and salt in a pot. Bring to a
boil on high heat; reduce heat to minimum and simmer until cooked,
approximately 45 minutes.

2 tbsp olive oil
2 cups onions, finely diced
1 tsp salt
2 tsp garlic, crushed
1 1/2 cups carrot, finely diced
1 cup celery, finely diced
1/4 cup dried tomato, finely diced
1/2 cup red pepper, diced
1/2 cup green pepper, diced
1 cup fresh parsley, finely chopped
1 cup green onion, finely sliced
1/2 cup chickpea cooking liquid

In a pot, heat olive oil; add diced onion and 1 tsp salt. Sauté two to
three minutes; add garlic. Stir, and a minute later add carrot, then
celery and diced tomato. Sauté until carrots are soft. Add red and
green peppers. A minute later, add parsley and green onion. Adjust
salt. Cook for an additional minute. Add cooked chickpeas.

In a bowl, combine cooked wild rice and chickpea mixture. Moisten
it with some of the reserved chickpea cooking liquid (approximately
1/2 cup).

Pastry
2 cups whole wheat pastry flour
pinch of salt
1/4 cup canola oil
1/4 cup olive oil
1/2 cup oat or soy milk (available at health food stores)

In a bowl, mix flour and salt with a fork. Add oil and oat or soy milk alternately while gently stirring with a fork.

Fill either 2 loaf pans or a 9x13 baking dish with the chickpea mixture. Roll out pastry, and cover loaves. Bake at 350°F until pastry is done, about 45 minutes. Serve with onion gravy.

Serves 6-8

Onion Gravy

2 tbsp olive oil
1 1/2 cups onion, sliced
1/2 tsp salt

Heat oil. Add onions and salt. Cook on low heat until onions are brown, but not burned (approximately 15 to 30 minutes).

Add: 1 cup vegetable stock or water, and bring to a boil.

Add: 1 bay leaf and a pinch of thyme. Let boil for a minute or two.

Add: 1 tbsp arrowroot dissolved in 1/2 cup water. Stir to thicken. Add 2 tbsp tamari.

Just before serving, add 1/4 cup diced green onions or chopped parsley.

Makes 1 1/2 cups

Ginger Cabbage

2 tbsp olive oil
2 cups sliced onions
2 cloves garlic
5-6 cups green cabbage *or* bok choy
1 cup carrot, cut in thin diagonal slices
1/2 tsp salt or to taste
pinch of cayenne
2 small red peppers, seeded and sliced
1 tsp grated ginger root

Slice cabbage.

In a wok (or wide-base saucepan), heat olive oil. Add onions and garlic and sauté for 5 minutes. Add cabbage, carrots, salt, and cayenne. Stir frequently, while cooking 5 minutes longer, or until cabbage is wilted and soft. Add red pepper and ginger just prior to serving.

Serves 8 - 10

Great Northern Bean Stew

1 cup great northern beans (soaked overnight, drained)
3 cups water
6 inch piece of kombu sea vegetable (optional)
2 tbsp olive oil
1 carrot, sliced diagonally
1 stalk celery, sliced diagonally
1 tsp salt

Place soaked beans in a pot and add 3 cups water. Bring to a boil on high heat, uncovered. Lower heat. Cover and let simmer 20-30 minutes. Beans should not yet be done.

In another pot, heat oil and sauté the onion, carrot, and celery until soft. Add salt. Do not brown. Cook only until vegetables are wilted.

Add beans and cooking liquid to sautéed vegetables and cook until beans are fully cooked, approximately 15-30 minutes longer. Kombu may be discarded before beans are added to sautéed vegetables, or sliced into thin strips and added to stew.

Adjust seasoning before serving.

Serves 6-8

Greek Leek Stew

1/2 cup olive oil
2-3 large leeks
1-2 carrots
2 stalks of celery or 1 small celeriac root, including leaves if available
2 cups potato, scrubbed or peeled, and cut in pieces
(small potatoes can be left whole)
1 cup diced fresh tomato
1 cup water
1-2 tsp salt or to taste

Wash and cut leeks into inch long rounds, including green portion. Cut carrots and celery into inch long pieces; include leafy portion of celery. You should have 5 cups of leeks and 1 cup each of carrots and celery.

Sauté leeks in olive oil for 5 minutes. Add carrot, celery (or celeriac) and cook for 10 minutes on medium heat. Add salt, tomato, and potato and cook for 25-30 minutes until potatoes are soft.

Serves 6

Green Lentil Stew

1 1/2 cups green lentils
6 cups water
1 onion, medium sized, diced
1 carrot, medium sized, diced
2 stalks celery, diced
3 bay leaves
3 cloves garlic
3 tbsp olive oil
1 tsp salt
3 inch piece of kombu sea vegetable (optional)
2 cups water or stock
1/2 cup chopped parsley

Bring green lentils and water to a boil. Cook for 5 minutes. Drain and discard cooking water. In a medium sized pot, heat olive oil, add diced onion and cook on medium heat for 5 minutes. Add diced carrot and celery and cook until soft. Add 2 cups water or stock, kombu, diced or crushed garlic, bay leaves and drained lentils. Cook for 10 minutes. Add 1 tsp salt and continue cooking until lentils are well done but not mushy. Serve topped with parsley.

Green Lentil Burdock Stew: 1-2 roots of burdock scrubbed and thinly sliced on the diagonal may be added to the pot with the onion.

Serves 8

Lasagna

12 whole wheat lasagna noodles
2 packages spinach, washed, cooked, drained, and chopped fine
2 tbsp olive oil
1 cup diced onions
1 tsp rubbed basil
1 tsp rubbed oregano
1 tsp salt
2 cups thinly sliced mushrooms
2 cups thick tomato sauce (canned or homemade)
2 blocks firm tofu (1 kg), crushed
1/4 cup tamari
1 cup grated cheddar cheese

Cook lasagna noodles in boiling water for 5 minutes; set aside. Cook spinach in 2 cups boiling water for 1-2 minutes; drain, chop and set aside. Crush tofu and mix with tamari; set aside. Grate cheese; set aside. In a pot, heat oil, add onions, basil, oregano and salt. When onions are soft, add mushrooms and cook for 10 minutes. Turn off heat and add the cooked chopped spinach, stirring well to mix. Drain through a colander and put aside.

Putting the Lasagna Together

In a lasagna pan put ingredients in layers as follows:

Layer		
	1	Tomato sauce (2/3 cup)
	2	Lasagna noodles (1/4 noodles)
	3	Tofu (1/2 batch)
	4	Grated cheese (thin layer)
	5	Noodles
	6	Spinach, mushroom, onion mixture
	7	Tomato sauce (2/3 cup)
	8	Noodles
	9	Tofu
	10	Cheese
	11	Noodles
	12	Tomato sauce
	13	Cheese (thin layer)

Bake at 300° F for 45-60 minutes, until lightly browned.

Makes 1 pan (12 large pieces)

Leek Basmati Casserole

Grain
1 cup white basmati rice
2 1/2 cups water
1/4 tsp salt

Wash and drain rice. Put into pot with water and salt. Bring to a boil on high heat. Reduce heat to simmer. Cover and cook for 20-25 minutes. Set aside.

Vegetables
2 tbsp olive oil
1 tsp dried rosemary *or* 1 tbsp fresh rosemary
1/2 tsp salt
3 cups thinly sliced leeks

In pot, heat olive oil. Add rosemary, leeks and salt and cook on medium heat until soft; about 7-10 minutes. Set aside.

6 cloves garlic
1 block firm tofu (400-500 g)
3 tbsp umeboshi paste
1 cup water
1/4 cup cashew butter

In a food processor, mix garlic, tofu, umeboshi paste, water and cashew butter until smooth.

To the leeks, add cooked rice and tofu-garlic mixture. Mash with a potato masher or wooden spoon until well mixed, Place in a glass casserole. Cover and bake at 350° F for 15-20 minutes.

Glaze
3/4 cup water
1 cup diced mixed vegetables (carrots, leek, turnip, squash)
or 1 cup sliced mushrooms *or* 1 cup diced scallions
1 tsp grated ginger root
1 tbsp arrowroot dissolved in 1/8 cup water
2 tbsp tamari

Bring water to a boil and add vegetables. Add ginger and tamari.
Boil again and add arrowroot mixture. Stir until thick. Pour over
casserole and serve.

Serves 8

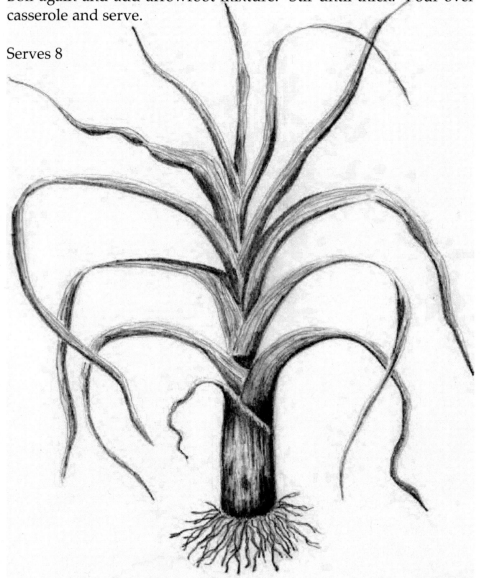

Mediterranean Green Beans

1 1/2 lbs green beans
1/4 cup olive oil
1 cup diced onion
1/4 cup water
3-4 cups chopped potato
1 cup fresh, diced tomato
1 clove garlic, crushed
1 tsp salt

Cut green beans into 1 inch pieces. You should have 4-5 cups. Sauté the onions in the olive oil. Add green beans and sauté together. Add water and cook for about 10 minutes. Add potato, tomato, garlic, and salt. Cook for 20-30 minutes, until the potatoes are soft.

Serves 4-6

Millet

2 cups millet
4 cups water
1/2 - 1 tsp salt

Wash millet very well in several changes of water. The millet is clean when the water is no longer cloudy. Drain through a fine sieve.

Place a wide, heavy bottomed pan on high heat. When millet is drained, add it to the pot, and stir with a wooden spoon. Pan roast on high heat for a few minutes, lowering the heat as the millet starts to dry out. Continue to stir well until the grains are dry and separate. They should not turn brown but start to become golden and smell aromatic. Add water all at once; add salt. Turn heat to low and cook for 15-20 minutes.

Serves 6-8

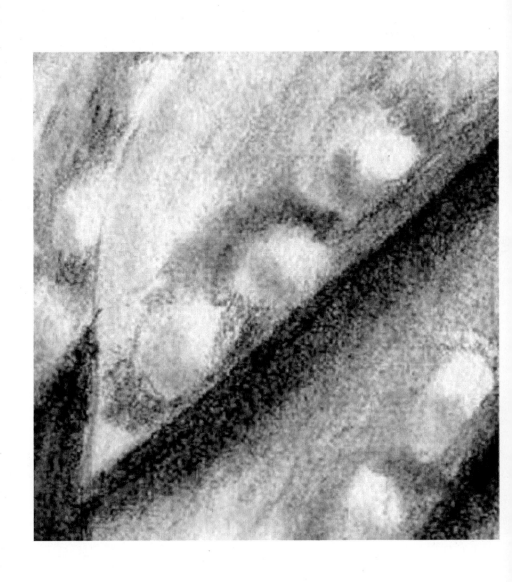

Minted Snow Peas

1 tbsp olive oil
1 clove garlic, crushed
4 cups snow peas, strings removed
1/4 - 1/2 tsp salt, or to taste
1/4 cup finely chopped fresh mint
1 cup diced green onions

In pan heat oil on high heat. Add garlic and cook for 1 minute. Do not allow to burn or brown.

Add snow peas and salt and cook until peas change colour (1-2 minutes) but are still crunchy. Peas should remain dark green.

Turn heat off and add mint and onions.

Cover. Wait one minute and serve.

Serves 8-10

Mixed Vegetable Curry

3-4 tbsp olive oil
2 tbsp ghee or butter (optional)

Spices

Pinch of asafœtida
1/4 tsp ground cumin
1/4 tsp ground coriander
1/2 tsp garam masala
1/4 tsp turmeric
1/8 tsp ground cardamom
1/4 tsp cayenne (add more for a hot curry, less for milder)

In a wide pot heat oil and, if used, ghee or butter. Add spices and toast on medium heat for 2-3 minutes, making sure not to burn them.

Add:
1 large onion, sliced thin
1 tbsp grated ginger root
1 tbsp garlic, crushed
Cook for 2 - 3 minutes. Do not let onion get soft.

Add:
1 cup carrot, thinly sliced on the diagonal
1 cup celery, thinly sliced on the diagonal
2-3 cups green beans, whole
2 cups thinly sliced cabbage
1/2 tsp salt

Turn heat on high and cook until vegetables change colour. Do not over cook. Vegetables should still be crisp. Top with:

1 red pepper, sliced
1/2 cup fresh coriander, chopped fine
juice of 1 lime
2 sliced tomatoes

Serves 8

Mixed Boiled Vegetables

2-3 carrots
1 bunch kale
1 cup Brussels sprouts
1 cup broccoli
1 cup cauliflower
6 cups water
1/4 cup olive oil
1/8 cup umeboshi plum vinegar

Boil water in a large pot. Add carrots and cook for 5 minutes. Add kale and Brussels sprouts and cook 10 minutes longer. Add broccoli and cauliflower and cook for a further 5 minutes. Drain and place in a bowl. Pour 1/4 cup olive oil and 1/8 cup umeboshi plum vinegar over them.

Serves 8-10

Mung Bean Curry

Soak 2 cups mung beans overnight in 8 cups water.

Drain.

Add one 4 inch piece of kombu and 4 cups fresh water. Bring to a boil, cover and cook for 30 minutes, or until soft.

In a pot heat 3 - 4 tbsp olive oil. Add the following spices:

pinch of asafoetida
1/2 tsp garam masala
1/4 tsp cayenne (may increase or decrease to taste)
1/4 tsp freshly ground cumin
1/2 tsp freshly ground coriander
1/2 tsp turmeric
1/4 tsp curry powder
1/4 tsp ground cardamom or 1-2 whole green cardamom pods

Cook spices in oil on low heat for 2 - 3 minutes. Stir frequently. Spices should roast gently to bring out their flavour; avoid burning.

Add:
1/2 cup onion, diced (optional)
1 tsp garlic, crushed
1 tsp salt

Cook for 5 minutes, or until onions are soft.

Add cooked mung beans and, if necessary, more water. Adjust water to obtain desired thickness.

Cook on minimum heat for 15 - 30 minutes longer. Turn heat off just before serving and add 1/2 cup fresh coriander finely chopped and the juice of 1 lemon.

1/2-1 cup diced tomato (optional) may be added with coriander.

Serves 10-12

Mushroom Stroganoff

1 tbsp olive oil
1 cup onion, diced
1/2 tsp salt
3 to 4 cups white mushrooms, washed and sliced
1 tbsp arrowroot flour
1 1/3 cups water
1 cup soft (silken) tofu (1/2 block)
2 tbsp umeboshi paste
1/4 cup cashew butter
1/4 cup lemon juice
fresh or dried tarragon or dill

Heat oil; add onion and salt. Cook for 3 to 5 minutes on medium heat until the onions are soft and translucent, but not brown. Add sliced mushrooms; cook until they are wilted and have released their liquid (5-7 minutes).

Meanwhile, dissolve arrowroot in 1/3 cup of water and set aside.

Make the creamy sauce: in a blender, mix tofu, 1 cup water, and umeboshi paste until very smooth. Add cashew butter; blend for a minute longer.

Add arrowroot mixture to mushrooms. Stir until thick. Add creamy sauce. Heat gently, but do not boil. Add lemon juice to taste. Add the tarragon or dill to taste. Serve over pasta or rice.

Serves 4-6

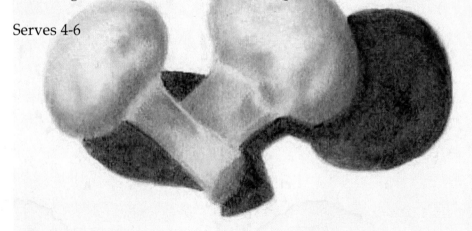

Navy Bean Stew

1 cup navy beans, soaked overnight in 6 cups water
4 inch piece of kombu seaweed
4 cups water
2 tbsp olive oil
1 medium onion, diced
1 large carrot, cut in half lengthwise, then in thin diagonal slices
1 celery stalk, cut into thin diagonal slices
pinch of salt
1/2 cup chopped parsley

Drain pre-soaked beans, place in 4 cups water with kombu and bring to a boil. Reduce heat to simmer and cook for 30 minutes.

In a pot, heat olive oil on medium-high. When olive oil is hot, add onions and sauté until soft. Add carrot and celery and cook just until vegetables have wilted. Add cooked beans with liquid. Add salt and continue to cook for 20 minutes, or until beans have fully cooked. Top with parsley

Serves 6-8

Okra and Potato Curry

3 potatoes, medium size, about one pound
4 cups okra, about 1 1/2 pounds
1/4 cup lemon juice
1 tsp salt

Scrub potatoes; cut into evenly sized pieces. Rinse and trim okra. Toss with lemon juice and salt. Set aside.

3 tsp olive oil
pinch asafœtida
1 tsp curry powder
2 tsp ground turmeric
1/4 tsp ground cardamom
fresh hot pepper, or cayenne pepper (optional)
1 tsp garam masala

Heat olive oil on very low heat. Add spices and roast gently for 2 to 3 minutes, making sure not to burn them.

Add:

2 cups onion, diced
1 1/2 tsp salt
1 tsp garlic, crushed
1/2 tsp fresh ginger root, grated

Cook for 2 to 3 minutes, then add:

1 cup fresh tomato, diced
1 1/2 cups water

Increase heat and bring to a boil. Add potatoes. Reduce heat and simmer for 20 minutes. Add okra (including lemon juice), simmer for 15 minutes longer. Adjust salt, if needed. Turn off heat. Garnish with 1 cup fresh diced tomato and 1/2 cup fresh chopped coriander leaves.

Serves 6-8

Olive Oil Mashed Potatoes

1 kg potatoes (6-7 medium sized potatoes), scrubbed or peeled and
   cut into chunks
1 tsp salt
water

Put potatoes in pot, cover with water, add salt and bring to a fast boil.
Reduce heat and cook until potatoes are soft. Drain. To drained potatoes add:

1/4-1/2 cup olive oil
1/2 cup chopped fresh dill
juice of one lemon

Mash potatoes well and add more salt if necessary. Sprinkle extra
dill on top and serve.

Serves 6

Oriental Vegetable Sauté

2 tbsp dark sesame or olive oil
3 leeks, cut into 1 inch lengths, including green parts
3 medium carrots, cut in half then into thin diagonal slices
1/2 cup hiziki sea vegetable, pre-soaked for 1/2 hour in 2 cups water
2 tbsp tamari

Heat oil. In wide pot, add leeks and carrots, cook on medium heat until leeks are soft. Add drained hiziki and tamari. Cook an additional 5 minutes. Serve.

Makes 8-10 servings

Potato Kale

6-7 medium potatoes (approximately 2 lbs)
water
1 tsp salt
1 bunch kale (organic)
3 tbsp butter
2 cups diced onions (leeks may be substituted)
1/2 - 1 cup half-and-half cream
1/2 - 1 cup whole milk
1/2 - 1 cup grated white medium cheddar cheese

Scrub potatoes and cut into small chunks. Place cut potatoes into a pot and add water to cover. Add salt. Put on high heat and bring to the boil. Reduce heat to minimum and cook until potatoes are soft. Drain.

In another pot, bring 2 litres of water to a boil. Add kale. Cook for 5 minutes. Kale must not be fully cooked. Drain and finely chop. Set aside.

In a third pot, melt butter and cook onions or leeks, with a pinch of salt, on medium heat until very soft. When cooked, add onion mixture to the pot of cooked, drained potatoes. Add cooked chopped kale, cream and milk, and mash together. Add salt to taste.

Place mashed mixture in a baking dish, sprinkle top with grated cheese and bake at 350° F until cheese is melted and top is light brown, about 20 minutes.

Makes 8 - 10 servings

Quinoa

2 cups quinoa grain
3 cups water
1 tsp salt

Wash quinoa 2-3 times in cold water. Strain through a sieve. Place drained quinoa in a pot, add water and salt. Bring to a fast boil on high heat, uncovered. Lower heat to minimum; cover and cook until soft and fluffy, about 20 minutes.

Serves 6-8

Quinoa is from South America. As it contains a natural soap to repel insect pests, it must be well washed before cooking. It is a low gluten grain and a quick alternative to rice.

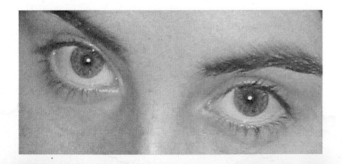

Ratatouille

1 large eggplant, 4 to 6 cups
1/2 tsp salt
4 or 5 zucchini (4 cups)
1 tsp olive oil
1/2 tsp salt

Cut eggplant into 1 1/2 inch cubes. Toss with salt. Spread on cookie sheet. Bake at 350° F for 45 minutes or until lightly browned.

Cut zucchini into one-inch rounds. Drizzle with olive oil and sprinkle with salt. Bake at 350° F for 30 minutes or until lightly baked but still firm.

1/4 cup olive oil
3 cups onions, sliced
1 tsp salt
1 tsp garlic, crushed
4 to 6 fresh tomatoes, sliced, or 1 cup tomato sauce
1 small red pepper, seeded and cut into large dice
1 small green pepper, seeded and cut into large dice
1 cup fresh Italian parsley, chopped
1 tsp dried rubbed basil, or 1/4 cup fresh basil
1 tbsp umeboshi vinegar

Heat oil. Add sliced onions and salt. Cook for 5 to 7 minutes on medium high heat. Add garlic and tomato. Cook for 7 to 10 minutes. Add eggplant, zucchini, parsley, and basil. Cook for 5 minutes. Do not overcook; vegetables should be firm. Add red and green pepper, and umeboshi vinegar. Heat until peppers are hot. Serve.

Serves 8-10

Red Lentil Dal

2 cups red lentils
5 cups water
1 tbsp olive oil (2 tbsp if no butter is used)
1 tbsp butter (optional)
1/4 tsp asafoetida
1/2 tsp garam masala
1/2 tsp cumin
1/4 tsp ground cardamom
1/4 tsp cayenne or 1 hot pepper, diced
2 cloves garlic
salt to taste
1/4 cup chopped fresh coriander

Cook red lentils in water until well done (30-45 min). Do not drain.

Heat oil and butter in medium size pot. Add spices and toast lightly. Add garlic and sauté until light brown. Add red lentils and salt; cook on low heat for 10 minutes. Garnish with chopped coriander and serve.

This will make a fairly thick dal. Add water for a thinner consistency.

Serves 8-10

Saffron Rice

1 tbsp butter
1 tbsp olive oil
6 allspice berries, whole
10 black peppercorns
1 cinnamon stick
10 cloves, whole
1/2 cup whole almonds, blanched
1 package saffron (1 g)
3 cups white basmati rice, washed well and drained
5-6 cups water
1 tsp salt or to taste
2 tbsp chopped fresh coriander (optional)

Heat oil and butter on medium-low heat. Add allspice, peppercorns, cinnamon, almonds and cloves. Reduce to low heat and toast for 2 minutes. Add washed rice and continue toasting with spices for an additional 5 minutes. Pour water over toasted mixture. Add salt and saffron. Return to high heat but reduce once fully boiling and simmer with lid on for about 20-25 minutes. May be served topped with chopped coriander.

Serves 8-10

Shepherd's Pie

Base
2 tbsp olive oil
1 cup onion, diced
1 small leek, diced, green leaves included
1/2 cup celery, diced
1/2 cup carrot, diced
1 large clove garlic, crushed
1/2 tsp dried rubbed basil
1/4 tsp dried rubbed oregano
1/4 tsp dried rubbed marjoram
1/2 cup fresh parsley, finely chopped
1 to 2 cups cooked beans, drained: chick peas, pinto beans, red kidney, navy, or your choice
1 1/2 cup tomato sauce, homemade or prepared
salt to taste (approximately 1 tsp)

Heat oil, add onions and leek. Sauté 5 minutes on medium high heat. Add celery, carrot, and garlic. Cook until vegetables are soft (5 - 7 minutes). Add basil, oregano, marjoram, parsley, beans, and tomato sauce. Add salt. Cook on medium heat 5-10 minutes, stirring periodically. Remove from heat.

Topping
1 pound potatoes
1 tsp salt
2 tbsp butter
1/2 cup milk
1/4 cup white medium cheddar cheese, grated

Scrub potatoes, cut into pieces, place in pot, cover with cold water; add salt. Bring to a boil on high heat, reduce to simmer, and cook until soft. Drain. Add butter, and enough milk to make a soft mixture. Mash. Add more salt if necessary.

Assembly
Empty bean mixture into a 9x9 inch glass pan. Spread potato mixture over the top. Sprinkle lightly with cheese. Bake at 350° F until cheese is melted and the top is nicely browned, 30-45 minutes.

Serves 6-8

Spiced Tofu

1 block firm tofu (400-500g), cut into 45 cubes: 3 x 3 x 5
1/3 cup olive oil
3 cloves garlic, crushed
1 tsp cumin seed whole
1/2 tsp cayenne or to taste
1 1/2 cups tomatoes, cut into small pieces
1 tsp salt
1 cup diced red or green pepper
1 tbsp umeboshi vinegar
1/2 cup fresh chopped coriander (optional)

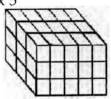

In wok, heat oil and sauté tofu until lightly brown.

Place tofu in colander or kitchen paper to drain off excess oil. Pour off excess oil from wok. Put cumin and cayenne in wok and cook for a few seconds on medium-low heat to bring out the flavour of the spices.

Add garlic and salt and cook 1-2 minutes longer.

Add tomatoes and cook until soft.
Add diced peppers and umeboshi vinegar.
Add tofu and stir until tofu is coated with the spicy sauce.

Coriander may be added before serving.

Serves 4-6

Spanakopita

Filling
4 packages fresh spinach *or* 3-3 1/2 cups cooked spinach (approximately)
2 tbsp melted butter
2 tbsp olive oil
2 cups chopped onion
1 tsp salt
2 cups chopped parsley
1 1/2 cups fresh dill, or 1/4 cup dried dill
2 cloves garlic, crushed
1 block firm tofu (400-500 g), mashed
1 cup feta cheese, crumbled
salt to taste
juice of 2 lemons

Wash spinach. Blanch in boiling water for 1-2 minutes. Drain, chop and set aside.

In a pan, heat butter and oil. Add onions and salt; cook until transparent. Add parsley, dill, garlic and cook until soft, about 5 minutes on high heat. Reduce heat to medium. Add mashed tofu, and chopped spinach, mixing well. Turn off heat, add feta cheese, lemon juice, and more salt if necessary. Pour contents of pan into a colander and allow to drain for 15 minutes.

Pastry
2 packages of filo pastry. If frozen, thaw by removing from freezer for two hours)
1/2 cup melted butter
1/2 cup olive oil

Melt butter in pot, add olive oil. Brush each sheet of filo lightly with the oil-butter mixture. Fold in half, brush again. Place a tablespoon of the mixture onto a corner of the folded sheet and roll/fold into triangles. Place on oiled cookie sheet. Bake at 350° F until light brown (about 20-30 minutes).

Makes 36 triangles.

Folding Instructions

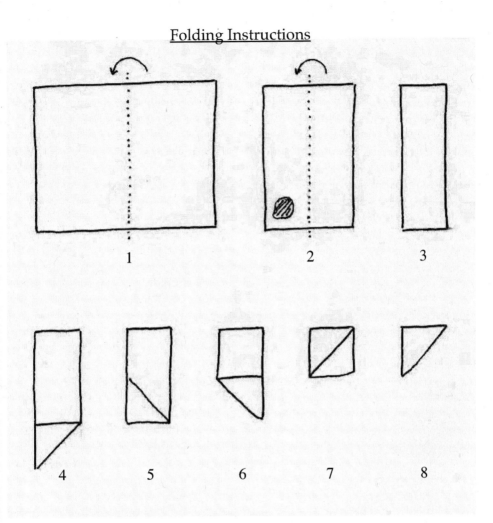

1 : brush sheet lightly with butter/oil; fold in half.

2, 3 : place filling in corner; fold in half; lightly brush with butter/oil.

4 : fold corner over filling.

5, 6, 7, 8 : continue folding

Brush top of triangle with butter/oil

Spicy Coriander Tempeh

1 package of tempeh (225 g)
2 cups water

Boil tempeh in 2 cups of water for 10 minutes. Drain. When cool, cut into 1 inch cubes. Set aside.

3 tbsp olive oil
1 cup sliced Spanish onion
1/4 tsp salt
1/2 tsp ground coriander
1/2 tsp ground cumin
2 cloves garlic, crushed
1/4 tsp cayenne
1/2 cup water
1/4 cup umeboshi vinegar
1/2 cup chopped fresh coriander
a few pieces of red and/or green pepper
1 diced tomato

Heat oil in pot, add onions and salt and cook on medium high heat for 3-5 minutes. Stir to avoid burning. Add ground coriander, cumin, garlic, cayenne and cook a little longer. Add tempeh and water and cook for 15 minutes. Add umeboshi vinegar, coriander, red and green pepper and tomato.

Serves 4

Spicy Eggplant

1 large eggplant; approximately one pound, yielding 4-5 cups when
   cubed into 1 1/2 inch pieces
1/2 tsp salt

Toss cubed eggplant with salt. Bake at 350° F for one hour, or until
lightly browned.

5 tbsp olive oil
3 cups onions, sliced
1/2 tsp salt
1 tsp fresh hot pepper, finely diced, *or* 1/2 tsp cayenne
1 tsp cumin seed, ground
2 cloves garlic, crushed
1 cup fresh tomato, diced
1 cup red pepper, diced
1 cup green pepper, diced
1/2 cup fresh coriander leaves
2 tbsp umeboshi vinegar

Heat oil; add sliced onions and salt. Sauté for ten minutes on medium heat. Add hot pepper or cayenne, cumin, and garlic. Add diced
tomato. Cook for two minutes longer. Add eggplant, red and green
peppers, fresh coriander, and umeboshi vinegar. Stir. Adjust salt to
taste.

Serves 6-8

Spicy Peanut Tempeh

2 packages of tempeh, frozen or fresh (225 g each)
2 cups water

Boil tempeh in water for 10 minutes. Drain. When cool enough to handle, cut into 1 inch squares. Set aside.

3 tbsp olive oil
1 large onion (1 cup) sliced
1 leek, washed and sliced diagonally, green part included
2 cups celery, sliced diagonally
1 cup carrot, sliced diagonally

Peanut Sauce
2 tsp garlic (2-4 large cloves)
1/2 cup lime or lemon juice
1/2 cup umeboshi vinegar
1 cup peanut butter
1 cup water
2 tsp ginger root
1/4 tsp cayenne or 1 hot pepper
1 cup fresh coriander

In a pot, heat oil on medium heat. Add onion, leek, celery and carrot. Cook for 5 minutes stirring to prevent from burning. Add cubed tempeh and cook for 5 minutes longer.

To prepare sauce: in a blender or food processor, grind garlic; add lime juice, vinegar, peanut butter, water, ginger and cayenne. Grind until smooth.

Pour sauce over tempeh and stir until bubbling hot.

Just before serving, add 1 cup diced fresh coriander. Adjust salt and lime juice if necessary.

Serve over noodles or rice.

Serves 8

Spinach Béchamel

Spinach: two 10-oz packages or 1 bunch fresh, yielding 2 cups cooked,
   drained, and chopped
3 tbsp butter
3 tbsp whole wheat pastry flour
1/4 cup half-and-half cream
1 cup boiling water
1/2 cup white medium cheddar cheese, grated
1 tsp salt

Wash and drain spinach. Blanch it briefly in boiling water. Drain.
Cool it quickly under cold water. Drain well, squeezing out excess
moisture. Blanching and cooling this way will retain good colour.
Turn it out onto a board; chop finely, and set aside.

On medium low heat, melt butter in saucepan. Add flour, and stir to
mix with the butter. Turn off heat. Add boiling water. Stir until
thickened. Add half-and-half cream. Whisk. Put on low heat. Add
1/4 cup grated cheese and salt. Cook on low heat one to two minutes. Add chopped spinach. Stir. Place in shallow glass pan (9x9
inches).

The recipe can be prepared in advance up to this point and stored,
under refrigeration, for up to 24 hours.

Sprinkle remaining cheese over top. Bake at 350° F until top is lightly
browned.

Serves 6

Stuffed Roasted Squash

1 squash (kuri, buttercup, Hubbard), approximately 2 kg

Stuffing
2 tbsp olive oil
2 cups diced Spanish onion
2 cloves garlic
1 cup thinly sliced leeks
1 cup thinly sliced celery
1 cup thinly sliced carrot
3 cups thinly sliced mushrooms
1/4 tsp each rubbed sage, thyme, savory, oregano
2 cups chopped parsley
1 tbsp fresh chopped basil or 1 tsp dried basil
2 cups whole wheat bread crumbs
1 tsp salt
1/8 cup tamari

In pan, heat oil, add onions and garlic and cook until soft. Add leeks, carrots, celery and cook for 5 minutes. Add mushrooms and cook an additional 5 minutes. Add, sage, thyme, savory, oregano, parsley and basil.

In a bowl, place bread crumbs. Add contents of pan and stir well. Add salt or tamari if needed.

Cut top off squash, take out seeds. Fill cavity with stuffing, place onto baking pan. Roast in medium (350° F) oven for 2 hours, or 400° F for 1 1/2 hours. Insert knife into squash to test for doneness. Knife should go in without resistance.

Alternate stuffing
Replace 2 cups breadcrumbs with 1 cup cooked wild or brown rice and 1 cup crushed tofu. This makes a more substantial stuffing.

Serves 10-12

Stuffed Tomatoes

2 cups arborio *or* white basmati rice
2 cups finely diced onions
2 cups finely chopped parsley, preferably flat leaf Italian type
1 1/2 cups finely chopped dill
1 cup finely chopped fresh mint *or* 3 tbsp dried rubbed mint
2 cloves garlic, crushed
1/2-1 cup olive oil
3 tbsp salt
1 cup water, or blended tomato pulp

In a large bowl wash and drain rice. Add remainder of ingredients and mix well.

Hollow out tomatoes and fill with stuffing. Do not over fill; leave a small space on top of each. Place in a pan deep enough so that tomatoes do not protrude over dish. Fill dish with water almost to the top of the tomatoes. Bake uncovered at 350° F for 1 1/2-2 hours or until done. Baste from time to time by pouring spoonfuls of the liquid from the pan over the tomatoes. By the time the tomatoes are done and the rice is fully cooked, most of the liquid will have evaporated.

Stuffing is sufficient for 12 large tomatoes

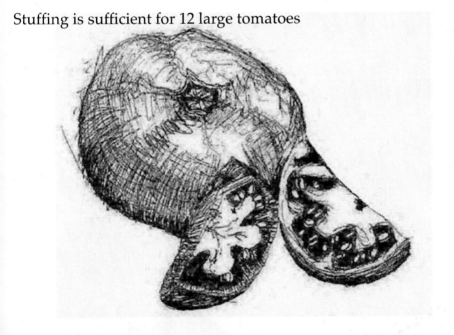

Tofu Cacciatore

1 block firm tofu
1/3 cup olive oil

In a wok, heat oil. Cut blocks of tofu into 45 squares (3 x 3 x 5). Fry in olive oil until brown on all sides. Drain and set aside.

Sauce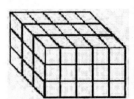
2 tbsp olive oil
1 cup diced onion
2 cloves garlic, crushed
1 cup diced carrot
1 cup diced celery
4 cups sliced mushrooms
1/2 cup finely chopped fresh basil *or* 1 tsp dried basil
1 tbsp fresh oregano, or 1 tsp dried oregano
3 bay leaves
2 cups tomato sauce, prepared or homemade
1 tsp salt
1 red pepper, diced
1 green pepper, diced
1 bunch finely chopped parsley

Heat oil in pan. Add onions and garlic and cook until soft. Add carrot, celery, mushrooms, basil, oregano, bay leaves and tomato sauce. Cook for 15-30 minutes. Add salt, tofu, red and green pepper and parsley. Adjust salt before serving if necessary.

Serves 6-8

Tofu Stir Fry

Vegetables and Tofu
1/3 cup olive oil
1 block of firm tofu cubed 3 x 3 x 5 (as on page 118)
1 cup carrots, thinly sliced diagonally
4-5 cups broccoli cut into florets, stems peeled and cut diagonally
1 bunch of green onions cut 1 inch long, including green parts
1 red pepper, seeded and thinly sliced
1 green pepper, seeded and thinly sliced

Sauce
1/2 cup water
1/4 cup tamari soy sauce
2 tsp fresh grated ginger root
4 cloves of garlic, crushed

Mix all ingredients in jar or bowl and set aside.

Glaze
1 tbsp arrowroot
1/4 cup water

Dissolve arrowroot in water.

Heat oil in wok. Sauté tofu on all sides in hot oil until evenly brown (10-15 minutes). Add sliced carrots and cook 2 minutes. Add broccoli stems and tops and stir until lightly cooked, 5-7 minutes. Add sauce, cook until broccoli is bright green but still firm. Add green onions and peppers, and arrowroot dissolved in water. Stir until thick. Vegetables must remain lightly cooked and crisp.

Serves 8-10

Turkish Leek Stew

1/4 cup olive oil
3 large leeks, sliced in 1/2 inch rounds
1 tsp salt
1 1/2 cups carrots in 1/2 inch rounds
2 cups celery in 1 inch lengths
2 cups water
1/2 cup basmati rice, washed
2 tbsp umeboshi vinegar

Heat oil in a pot and add leeks and salt. Sauté for 5 minutes. Add carrots and celery and cook for 5 minutes longer. Add water and rice and bring to a boil. Cover and simmer for 15-20 minutes or until rice is done. Add umeboshi vinegar and serve.

Serves 6-8

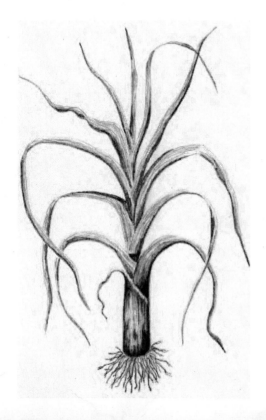

Turnip Fries

1 to 2 tbsp olive oil
1 rutabaga (yellow turnip), medium sized, cut into french-fry
sticks; about 2 cups
3 green onions, cut into 1 1/2 inch lengths
a garnish of fresh parsley, finely chopped
1/4 tsp salt (or to taste)

optional: a small carrot, cut into small julienne sticks
         a stalk or two of bok choy, sliced in 2 inch diagonals

In a wide-based saucepan, heat olive oil. Add rutabaga and
saute for 7 to 10 minutes, stirring frequently, until lightly
browned. The cooking time will depend upon the heat and the
size of turnip sticks. Test for doneness with a paring knife. When
almost cooked, add the green onions, parsley, salt. The carrots and
bok choy are added now as well. Saute and stir for one more
minute.

Turnip-Leek Sauté

1/4 cup dry hiziki seaweed, soaked in 2 cups cold water for one hour
3 tbsp olive oil
4 cups thinly sliced leeks
4 cups chopped rutabaga (yellow turnips) cut into french-fry shaped
    sticks
salt to taste
1 carrot, sliced thinly

Heat oil in wide pot. Add leek and sauté until wilted. Add turnip and 1/2 tsp salt. Cook at medium heat, stirring frequently. Add carrot and cook covered, on low heat, for 10 minutes. Drain hiziki and add to pot. Stir; adjust for salt if necessary.

Serves 6

Turnip Masala

1 or 2 large rutabaga (turnip), 1 inch cubes, approximately 3 cups.
Potatoes, cut into small chunks, approximately 2 or 3 cups
2 tbsp olive oil
1 tsp salt

Place turnip cubes into bowl. Toss with 1 tbsp olive oil and 1/2 tsp
salt. Spread onto cookie sheet. Roast at 350 degrees for 30 to 45
minutes until cooked and very slightly browned.
Toss potato pieces with 1 tbsp olive oil and 1/2 tsp salt. Spread on
a cookie sheet and lightly roast in the oven simultaneously with
the turnip.

2 tbsp olive oil and / or butter
a pinch of asafoetida
1 tsp ground cumin
1 tsp ground coriander
1 tsp ground turmeric
1/2 tsp garam masala
1/4 tsp ground cardamom
2 cloves garlic, crushed
1 fresh hot chili, or 1/2 to 1 tsp cayenne
1 cup chopped onions
1 cup coconut milk
1 cup water

Place butter and oil in pot on low heat. Add asafoetida, cumin,
coriander, turmeric, garam masala and cardamom. Toast spices in
the pot to bring out flavour. Stir frequently to prevent over-cooking.
Add crushed garlic and chopped chili pepper. Cook 2 to 3 minutes.
Add chopped onion. Continue to cook on low heat until onion is
soft, approximately 5 minutes. Add coconut milk and water. Bring
to a boil. Cook 5 minutes. Add roasted turnips and potatoes. Stir
gently, not to break vegetables.

Add 1/2 cup chopped fresh coriander leaves.
Taste. Adjust for salt.

Yield: 4 to 6 servings

Vegetable Quiche

Crust

2 cups soft whole wheat flour
pinch of salt
1/2 cup corn or canola oil
1/2 cup water

Place flour and salt in mixing bowl. Using a fork to mix pie crust, stir oil and water alternately into flour to form ball of dough. DO NOT overwork; mixture should be soft. Do not worry if dough appears to be marbled or unmixed, this will work itself out in the rolling.

Roll out onto waxed paper. Place rolled-out crust onto 9 inch pie plate, fluting the edges with fingers. Prick bottom and sides. Bake (partially cook) for 7 minutes at 350° F. Remove from oven and sprinkle a little grated cheese on crust.

Filling

2 tbsp butter
1 cup diced onion
1 1/2 cups thinly sliced mushrooms
1 1/2 cups finely chopped broccoli, or zucchini, or asparagus
1 tsp salt
3 eggs
1 cup (250 ml) half-and-half cream
1 cup (250 ml) whole milk
grated cheddar cheese
sprinkling of nutmeg
diced red and green pepper

In pan melt butter, add onions and salt. Cook on medium heat, stirring frequently, until soft but not brown. Add mushrooms and continue cooking until soft. Turn heat to high. Add broccoli (or zucchini or asparagus) and cook 1-2 minutes (long enough for broccoli to change colour to dark green). Remove from heat and drain into colander.

In large bowl beat eggs, add cream and milk. Place drained broccoli mixture into quiche shell and pour the egg/cream mixture over broccoli. Sprinkle with cheese and diced pepper and bake for 1 hour at 350° F (until golden).

Serves 8

Wild Rice Pilaf

2 cups wild rice
4 cups water
1/2 tsp salt

Wash rice and place in pot. Add water and salt and bring to the boil on high heat. Reduce heat to minimum. Cover pot and cook for 45 minutes until rice is done.

2 tbsp olive oil
1 onion, diced
1 carrot, diced
2 stalks celery, diced
1 zucchini, diced
1 clove garlic, crushed
1 tbsp dried, rubbed marjoram
1/2 tsp thyme
1 cup chopped parsley

Heat oil and cook onion until soft. Add garlic and cook 2 minutes longer. Add carrot, celery, marjoram, and thyme. Add cooked rice and stir to mix. Serve topped with fresh parsley.

Serves 6-8

Variation: substitute 1 cup of wild rice for 1 cup of other rice, such as: brown, wehani, brown or white basmati, country wild, or other.

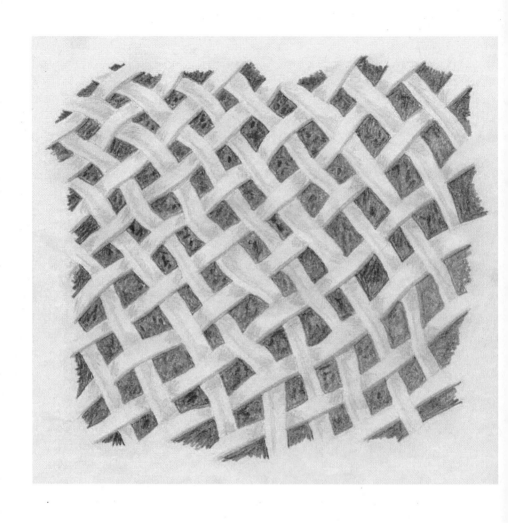

Desserts

Almond Raisin Squares

Base
3 cups almonds
2/3 cup barley flour
1/3 cup canola oil
1/3 cup maple syrup
1 tsp vanilla
1/3 cup apple cider

In a food processor, grind almonds until mixture looks like coarse breadcrumbs. Empty into a bowl, add barley flour and mix. In a separate bowl, mix oil, maple syrup, vanilla, and apple cider. Add wet ingredients to dry. Combine well.

Press mixture onto bottom of a 9 x 13 inch glass pan lined with parchment paper. If parchment paper is not available, oil and flour the pan.

Filling
2 cups Thompson or sultana raisins
2 cups water
2/3 cup tahini
1/3 cup canola oil
1 tbsp umeboshi paste
2/3 cup pecans
1/3 cup barley malt
2/3 cup maple syrup
1 tsp vanilla
2/3 cup arrowroot flour

Boil raisins in water for 5 minutes. Drain, reserving liquid.

In a food processor or blender, mix tahini, oil, umeboshi paste, maple syrup, barley malt, vanilla, arrowroot and raisin water. Blend until smooth. Add pecans and blend 1 minute longer. Spread raisins over crust. Pour contents of blender over raisins. Bake at 350° F for one hour until top is almost set; it will set further as it cools. When cool, cut into 24 squares.

Apple Strudel

10 cups sliced apples
1 cup raisins
1/2 cup water
1/3 cup unsalted butter (melted)
1 package filo pastry

Cook the apples and raisins in the 1/2 cup of water until soft. Take off heat and cool to room temperature.

Using one sheet of filo at a time, do the following:

-brush each sheet with butter, fold in half and brush with butter again

-place one large spoonful of apple mixture at the end of the folded filo in the center

-fold the 2 sides toward the center over the filling, brush with butter and roll up.

Brush tops lightly with butter and bake at 350° F for 30 minutes.

Makes 18 individual strudels. Refer to drawing overleaf.

Baklava

1 package filo pastry
1/3 cup unsalted butter (melted)
4 cups chopped almonds or walnuts
1–2 tsp cinnamon
1 tsp cardamom
1/2 cup maple syrup

Chop nuts and mix with cinnamon, cardamom, and maple syrup. Brush each filo sheet with butter and fold in half.

Brush again and place 1–2 tbsp filling on one end of the folded sheet. Fold ends in and roll like a cigar. Place in baking pan one inch apart from each other and bake at 350° F for 20 - 30 minutes, or until golden.

Remove from oven. Drizzle maple syrup over each piece. Let cool before serving.

Makes 18-20 pastries

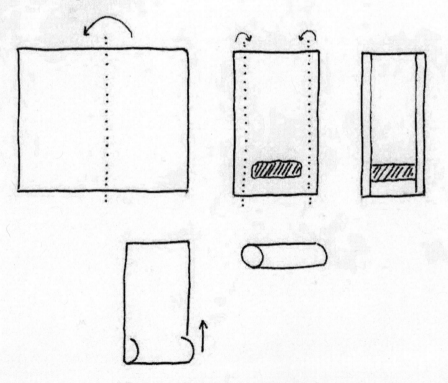

Banana-Coconut Cake

Dry Ingredients
4 1/2 cups soft wheat or spelt flour
3 tsp baking powder
pinch of salt
1/2 cup shredded coconut

Wet Ingredients
2/3 cup corn or canola oil
2/3 cup maple syrup
2 cups pineapple juice
1 tsp vanilla
3 bananas, thinly sliced

Topping
1/2 cup shredded coconut
2 tbsp rice malt

Mix all dry ingredients. Mix all wet ingredients. Combine dry and wet ingredients. Fold sliced bananas into cake mixture. Pour into 9 inch tube pan. Top with shredded coconut mixed with rice malt. Bake at 350° F for 45-60 minutes.

Serves 8-10

Blueberry Cake

Dry Ingredients
2 cups spelt flour
3 tsp baking powder
1 tsp cinnamon
pinch of salt

Wet Ingredients
1/2 cup corn *or* canola oil
1/2 cup maple syrup
1/2 cup blueberries, fresh or frozen
1/2 cup soymilk, or fruit juice
1 tsp pure vanilla extract

In a bowl, mix together dry ingredients. In a second bowl, whisk together wet ingredients. Pour wet ingredients onto dry. Stir to combine. Pour into oiled and floured 9 inch tube pan. Bake at 350° F for 45 to 60 minutes, until inserted knife comes out clean. Allow to cool in pan for 5 minutes. Turn onto cake rack. Let cool for one hour.

Serve topped with cream cheese icing (see p 143) or blueberry glaze.

Serves 8-10

Blueberry Glaze

1 cup apple or apple-blueberry juice
1 1/2 cups blueberries, fresh or frozen
2 tbsp arrowroot
4 tbsp maple syrup

Bring juice to a boil. Add 1 cup of blueberries; return to boil. To the boiling liquid, add arrowroot dissolved in maple syrup. Stir for a minute while it thickens. Remove from heat; add the last 1/2 cup of blueberries. Serve over cake.

Blueberry Pie

Nut Crust
1 cup large flake rolled oats
1/2 cup almonds
1 cup barley flour
1/4 tsp cinnamon
a pinch of salt
1/3 cup corn or canola oil
1/3 cup maple syrup

Filling
4 cups blueberries, fresh or frozen
1/4 cup agar flakes
2 cups blueberry juice or apple juice
1/3 cup arrowroot
1/4 cup maple syrup

Oil and flour one 10 inch pie plate. In food processor grind oats, almonds, salt and cinnamon. In a bowl, mix the flour with the contents of the food processor. Add the oil and maple syrup and mix into a soft dough. Press into the pie plate and flute the edges. Bake at 350° F for 25 minutes until golden brown. Allow to cool while preparing filling.

Mix the arrowroot and maple syrup in a small bowl and set aside. Heat the blueberry juice and agar and stir until the juice boils and the agar is fully dissolved. Add 2 cups of blueberries and boil again. Add maple syrup and arrowroot to boiling blueberries and juice and stir until slightly thick. Turn off heat. Add the remaining 2 cups of blueberries and mix well. Pour into baked crust and refrigerate until set: about 2 hours.

Serves 8

Bran Muffins

Dry Ingredients
2 cups spelt or wheat flour
1 cup spelt or wheat bran
3 tsp baking powder
1 tsp cinnamon
pinch of salt

Wet Ingredients
1/2 cup corn or canola oil
1/2 cup maple syrup
1/2 cup chopped apple
1 banana, thinly sliced
1 cup soymilk or fruit juice
1 tsp pure vanilla extract

In a bowl, mix together dry ingredients. In a second bowl, whisk together wet ingredients. Pour wet ingredients onto dry. Stir to combine. Spoon into either oiled or paper-lined muffin tins. Bake at 375° F for 20 minutes.

Makes 12 muffins

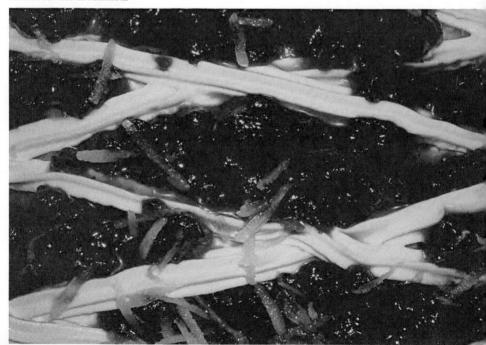

Cashew Creme

1 cup raw cashews, whole or pieces

Soak in 3 cups of water for 3 hours or more. Drain. Blend until smooth with:

1/2 cup water
1 tbsp maple syrup
1 tbsp vanilla
1 tbsp lemon juice

Use in place of whipped cream.

Carob Walnut Chews

Base
1 1/2 cups large-flake rolled oats
1 cup almonds
1/4 cup coconut
1/4 cup carob powder
1 cup barley flour
pinch of salt
1/2 cup corn oil
1/2 cup maple syrup

In food processor grind oats, almonds and coconut. Add carob powder. Process 1 minute longer. Place contents of food processor into a bowl. Add barley flour and salt. Mix oil and maple syrup, pour over dry ingredients and mix well. Line a 9 x 13 inch pan with parchment paper and press mixture into it.

Topping
1 cup carob chips
2 cups walnuts
1 1/2 cups coconut
1 cup rice malt
1/4 cup barley malt
1 tbsp vanilla
1/4 block soft tofu
1/4 tsp salt
1/3 cup arrowroot powder

In a large bowl place carob chips and coconut. Place the rest of ingredients except for walnuts in food processor. Process for 1 - 2 minutes, until everything is well blended. Add walnuts and blend a few seconds longer. Pour over base and bake at 350° F for 45-60 minutes or until light brown. It will set as it cools.

Makes 24 medium sized pieces.

Coconut Dream Squares

Base
1 1/2 cups large flake rolled oats

Grind oats in a food processor until they resemble fine breadcrumbs. Empty into a bowl.

1 cup spelt flour
1 1/2 cups barley flour
1/2 cup corn oil and 1/2 cup maple syrup for binding
pinch of salt
1/2 cup unsweetened, desiccated coconut

Add spelt, barley flour, salt, coconut. Mix. Add oil and maple syrup and pour into flour mixture. Mix to a cookie dough consistency. Press into a 9 x 13 inch pan that has been lined with parchment paper.

Topping
2 cups rice malt, slightly above room temperature
juice of 1 lemon
1/2 plus 1/8 cup arrowroot powder
1/2 tbsp vanilla
1/2 tbsp umeboshi paste
1/2 block firm tofu
3 cups coconut
1 cup raisins
1 1/2 cups coarsely ground walnuts

In a food processor, combine rice malt, lemon juice, arrowroot powder, vanilla, umeboshi paste and tofu. Blend until creamy and very smooth. Combine contents of food processor with coconut, raisins and walnuts. Pour combined mixture onto crust.

Bake for 1 hour and 20 minutes at 325° F or until golden. Score into squares before it cools. Let cool completely before lifting out of pan.

Makes 24 squares.

Cheese Cake

Crust
1 1/2 cups almonds
1/4 cup maple syrup
1/4 cup apple juice, or cider
1/4 cup corn oil
1/2 cup barley flour
pinch of salt

Grind almonds in food processor. In a bowl mix barley flour, salt and ground almonds. Stir well. Add maple syrup, corn oil, and apple juice, and mix by hand to form a ball of dough. Press dough out into the base of a 6-7 inch cheesecake pan.

Filling
3 eggs
2/3 cup sucanat (unrefined cane sugar)
1/2 kg cream cheese
1 tsp vanilla
1/3 cup apple cider

Blend all filling ingredients in a food processor until very smooth. Pour onto crust base and bake at 350° F for 25-30 minutes, or until top is light brown. Let cool before serving.

Makes 8 pieces

Chocolate Almond Fudge

1 cup raw almonds
1 cup chocolate chips, dairy-free
1 cup of rice syrup
1 cup almond butter
1 cup raw sunflower seeds
1 cup sesame seeds
1 tsp orange rind
3 tbsp freshly squeezed orange juice
1 tsp pure vanilla extract

Place almonds on a cookie sheet. Toast in oven at 350° F for about 15 minutes, or until lightly browned. Chop in food processor, or by hand, until they resemble coarse bread crumbs.

In a double boiler, heat rice syrup and chocolate chips until chips have melted. Add the rest of the ingredients. Stir with wooden spoon until well mixed.

Line a 9 x 13 inch pan with parchment paper. Scrape fudge into pan; press with spatula or fingers to an even thickness. Let cool for 15 minutes. Score into squares. Refrigerate until completely cool.

Chocolate Cake

Dry Ingredients
2 cups soft whole wheat flour
pinch of salt
1 tbsp baking powder
1 cup cocoa powder

Wet Ingredients
1 cup apple juice
1/2 cup apple sauce
1 cup maple syrup
2 tbsp canola or corn oil
1 tsp vanilla

Mix dry ingredients very well. Combine wet ingredients in a separate bowl. Add wet to dry ingredients. Combine well. Pour batter into two 10 inch, oiled and floured layer pans and bake at 350° F for 25-30 minutes until knife comes out clean. Let cool.

Icing
3/4 cup cashew butter
1/2 cup water
2 tsp vanilla
1/2 cup maple syrup
1/2 cup cocoa powder
200 g (1 cup) soft (silken) tofu
2 tbsp apricot preserve

Boil tofu in water to cover for 2 minutes before blending. In a blender or food processor, blend all ingredients until smooth. Spread 1/4 of the icing between the two layers of cake. Use remainder of icing to ice top and sides of cake.

Serves 16

Chocolate Chip Muffins

Dry Ingredients
2 cups spelt flour
1/2 cup oat bran
1/2 cup cocoa powder
1 cup naturally sweetened chocolate chips, organic if possible
1 tsp cinnamon
2 tsp baking powder
pinch of salt
Wet Ingredients
1/2 cup corn *or* canola oil
1/2 cup maple syrup
1 tsp vanilla
1 banana, thinly sliced
1 cup soymilk

In a bowl, mix together dry ingredients. In a second bowl, whisk together wet ingredients. Pour wet ingredients onto dry. Stir to combine. Spoon into either oiled or paper-lined muffin tins. Bake at 375° F for 20 minutes.

Makes 12 muffins

To make Double Chocolate Muffins, double the number of chocolate chips.

Cocoa-Banana Pie

Rice Crust
3/4 cup raw almonds
3/4 cup brown rice flour
1/3 cup canola oil
1/3 cup maple syrup
pinch of salt
1/4 tsp cinnamon

In a food processor, grind the almonds until they resemble bread crumbs. In a bowl, mix ground almonds, rice flour, salt and cinnamon. In another bowl, mix oil with maple syrup. Combine wet and dry ingredients. Press into an oiled and floured 9 1/2 or 10 inch pie plate. Bake at 350° F until lightly browned, approximately 25 minutes. Allow to cool.

Filling
1 litre (4 cups) cocoa soymilk
1/4 cup agar flakes
1/2 cup maple syrup
1/3 cup arrowroot flour
1 tsp vanilla extract
2 bananas, or 3 cups sliced banana

Bring soymilk and agar to a boil on medium heat. Stir frequently to prevent burning. Reduce heat and simmer until agar is completely dissolved.

Mix arrowroot into the maple syrup; whisk it into simmering soymilk mixture until thick. It will thicken almost immediately. Remove from heat. Allow to cool for 15-30 minutes. Meanwhile, slice bananas into pie shell. Stir vanilla extract into soymilk mixture, then pour it over the sliced bananas. Allow to set in refrigerator for 2 to 3 hours.

Serves 8-10

Lemon Cranberry Coconut Square

crust

1/2 cup rolled oats, finely ground
1/2 cup spelt flour
1/2 cup barley flour
1/2 tsp salt
1/4 cup canola oil
1/4 cup maple syrup

Preheat oven to 350 degrees. Mix all dry ingredients together in a bowl. In a second bowl, whisk together the oil and maple syrup. Add wet to dry. Mix well.
Use an 8 inch by 8 inch square baking pan. Either oil the pan or line it with parchment paper. Press the crust evenly into the pan. Bake for 10 minutes.

filling

1/4 block firm tofu
3 medium sized lemons, both juice and rind
1 tsp umeboshi plum paste
1 cup rice syrup
1/2 cup arrowroot flour
1 tsp vanilla
1 1/2 cups unsweetened dessicated coconut
1 cup cranberries

In a food processor, blend tofu, lemon juice, zested rinds and umeboshi paste until smooth. Scrape down the sides of the food processor with a spatula. Add the rice syrup, arrowroot and vanilla. Blend until smooth.
Place coconut and cranberries in a separate bowl. Add the liquid mixture. Stir well.

Pour the filling onto the pre-baked crust.
Bake for 30 to 40 minutes, until the top surface is golden brown and slightly puffed.

Yield: one 8 by 8 pan; 12 to 16 squares

Lemon Coconut Cake

Dry Ingredients
3 cups spelt flour
1/2 cup unsweetened desiccated coconut
3 tsp baking powder
pinch of salt

Wet Ingredients
3/4 cup canola oil
3/4 cup maple syrup
1 1/3 cups vanilla soy milk
1/2 cup freshly squeezed lemon juice
2 tsp grated organic lemon rind

In a bowl, mix together dry ingredients. In a second bowl, whisk together wet ingredients. Pour wet ingredients onto dry. Stir to combine. Pour into oiled and floured 9-inch tube pan. Bake at 350° F for 45 to 60 minutes, until inserted knife comes out clean. Allow to cool in pan for 5 minutes. Turn onto cake rack. Let cool for one hour.

Serve topped with cream cheese icing or a lemon glaze. Sprinkle with toasted coconut.

Serves 10-12

Cream Cheese Icing

8 ounces cream cheese
1 tsp pure vanilla extract
1 tsp lemon rind
1/4 cup maple syrup

Blend all ingredients in food processor, or whisk by hand. Pour over cake.

Lemon Glaze

1 cup apple juice
1 tbsp agar flakes
2 tbsp arrowroot
1/3 cup lemon juice
1 tsp organic lemon rind
1/2 cup maple syrup

Boil agar in apple juice until agar flakes are fully dissolved. Mix arrowroot into lemon juice, maple syrup, and lemon rind; pour into boiling liquid. Stir until lightly thickened. This will take only a minute or two. Allow to cool for 10 minutes. Pour over cake.

Toasted Coconut

Place 1/2 cup of unsweetened dessicated coconut onto a pie plate. Toast in an oven at 300° F for 10 minutes. Be watchful, as coconut will burn very quickly. Allow to cool for a few minutes; sprinkle over cream cheese icing.

Lemon Tofu Cheesecake

Crust
1 cup large flake oats
1 cup pecans
1 cup barley flour
a pinch of salt
1/4 tsp cinnamon
1/2 cup canola or corn oil
1/2 cup maple syrup

In a food processor, grind oats for 1-2 minutes. Add pecans and grind a little longer until mixture resembles coarse breadcrumbs. Empty oats and pecans into a bowl. Add barley flour, salt, and cinnamon and mix well. Add oil and maple syrup and mix with hands to form a soft dough. Press evenly into a 10-12 inch spring form pan that has been oiled and floured. Bake at 350° F for 20 minutes.

Filling
1 1/2 blocks (750 g) soft (silken) tofu
1/2 cup almond butter
3/4 cup lemon juice
2 tsp lemon rind
1/3 cup apple juice
2 tbsp arrowroot
2 tsp vanilla
1/2 cup maple syrup
pinch of salt

Blend filling ingredients in food processor until smooth. Pour into partially baked crust. Return to oven and bake for a further 30 minutes.

Glaze
1 cup apple juice
1 tbsp agar flakes
1 tbsp arrowroot
1/4 cup lemon juice
1/4 cup maple syrup
1 tsp lemon rind

In a pot, heat apple juice and agar. Cook until agar is completely dissolved. Mix remaining ingredients together in a cup and stir to mix well. Add to boiling pot and cook for a minute to thicken. Allow to cool for a few minutes. Pour over baked tofu cheesecake and allow to cool until cheesecake has set (2-3 hours).

Makes either one 12-inch spring-form, or one 9x13 inch pan

Fresh Fruit Torte

Base
1 cup large flake rolled oats
1/2 cup unsweetened shredded coconut
1 cup barley flour
1/4 tsp cinnamon
pinch of salt
1/3 cup corn oil
1/3 cup maple syrup

Filling
1 block firm tofu (400-500 g)
1/2 cup almond butter
1/2 cup maple syrup
3 bananas
2 tbsp vanilla
1/4 tsp salt

Glaze
1/2 cup apple juice
1 cup blueberries
1 tbsp arrowroot
1/4 cup apple juice
sliced kiwi or other fruit for garnish

Grind oats in food processor then add other dry ingredients. Add oil and maple syrup. Press into the bottom of a 10-inch layer cake pan. Bake at 350° F for 10-15 minutes. Cool.

Mix the filling ingredients in the food processor and spread it over the partially cooked crust. Bake at 350° F for a further 20-25 minutes. Cool.

Dissolve the arrowroot in the 1/4 cup apple juice and set aside. Heat the 1/2 cup of juice on high heat, add 1/2 cup blueberries and bring to a boil. Add the arrowroot mixture: the juice and berries will thicken immediately. Turn off heat and add another 1/2 cup of blueberries. Set aside to cool and thicken.

Garnish the baked torte with kiwi on the outer edge and pour the blueberry glaze in the center.

Millet Custard

1 cup millet
4 cups water
4 cups apple juice
pinch of salt
4 cups applesauce
3 tsp lemon rind
3/4 cup lemon juice
1/2 cup cashew butter

Wash millet. Drain. Add water, apple juice and salt, and bring to the boil on high heat. Turn heat to minimum, place heat dispenser under pot and continue to cook on low heat for 45-60 minutes. Take pot off heat.

To pot of cooked millet add apple sauce, rind and juice of lemons, and cashew butter. Mix well with spoon or spatula.

Blend in small batches divide this quantity into 4 parts for the blender. Pour into a bowl large enough to hold the entire amount. It will be liquid but will thicken as it cools. Allow 2-3 hours to set.

Serves 8-10

Mocha Walnut Cake

Dry Ingredients
1 cup whole wheat pastry flour
3 cups unbleached flour
1/4 tsp salt
4 tsp baking powder
1 cup walnuts chopped
1/2 cup grain coffee powder

Wet Ingredients
1/2 cup corn oil
3/4 cup maple syrup
1/2 cup soy milk
1 3/4 cup apple juice
2 tsp vanilla

Mix wet ingredients.
Mix dry ingredients.
Combine wet and dry ingredients. Pour into oiled and floured layer cake pans or tube pan.
Bake at 350° F for 35-40 minutes.

Mocha Icing
250 g (1/2 block) tofu (silken)
1/4 cup maple syrup
1 tbsp cashew butter (may substitute almond butter or tahini)
pinch salt
1/2 cup grain coffee powder

Blend all ingredients.

Serves 8-10

Orange Cardamom Cake

Dry Ingredients
3 cups soft wheat or spelt flour
2 tsp baking powder
1 tsp cardamom
pinch of salt

Wet Ingredients
1/2 cup corn oil
1/2 cup maple syrup
5 tsp orange rind
1 cup orange juice
1/2 cup apple juice
2 tsp vanilla

In large bowl big enough to mix cake, place dry ingredients. In another bowl measure wet ingredients. Combine wet and dry. Pour cake batter into oiled and floured tube pan and bake at 350° F for 45–60 minutes. Test cake with toothpick or sharp knife. Let cool for 10 minutes in pan, then take out of pan and cool on wire rack. Serve warm or with orange glaze.

Glaze
2/3 cup orange juice
1/2 cup apple juice
1/4 cup maple syrup
2 tsp orange rind
2 tbsp arrowroot
roasted, chopped almonds (optional)

Combine arrowroot and maple syrup. In a pot, heat orange and apple juices and orange rind. When the juice comes to a boil, add arrowroot and maple syrup. Cook until clear. This will take 1-2 minutes. Remove from heat and allow to cool. Glaze top of cake; sprinkle with roasted chopped almonds.

Serves 8-10

Peanut Butter Cookies

Dry Ingredients
3 cups whole wheat flour
1/8 tsp salt
1/2 tsp baking powder

Wet Ingredients
1 cup peanut butter, crunchy or smooth
1/3 cup corn oil
1/2 cup maple syrup
1/2 cup rice malt
1 tsp vanilla

In a bowl combine the wet ingredients.

In a separate bowl, sift flour, salt, and baking powder. Add wet ingredients to dry and mix well.

Drop spoonfuls of the batter onto parchment paper lined cookie sheets and flatten into shape with a fork.

Bake at 350° F until lightly browned, approximately 20 minutes. The cookies should be dry and golden on top but still soft on the bottom. They will harden as they cool.

Makes two dozen cookies.

Pecan Pie

Pie Crust
1 Nut Crust (see page 133)

Filling
1 1/3 blocks firm tofu
2 cups pecans
1 cup rice syrup (or 1 1/4 cups for a sweeter pie)
1/4 cup barley malt
1 tbsp vanilla
2 tbsp lemon juice
1/8 tsp salt
1/4 cup arrowroot
1/2 cup orange juice
1 tsp orange rind

Oil and flour a 9 inch pie plate. Pat crust dough into plate; flute. Do not cook.

Grind pecans in food processor then add arrowroot; blend. Add tofu; blend, then add remaining ingredients. Pour filling into unbaked pie shell, decorate with 8-10 pecans (1 per serving). Bake at 350° F for 1 hour and 15 minutes.

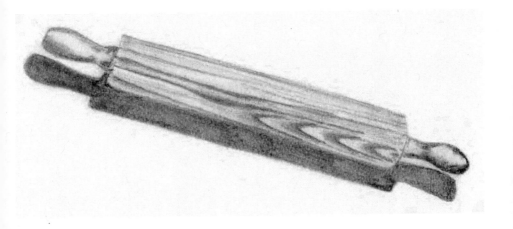

Pumpkin Pie

Pastry
2 cups soft whole wheat pastry flour
1/2 tsp salt
1/2 cup corn oil
1/2 cup cold water

In a bowl, mix flour and salt with a fork. Add oil and water alternately while gently stirring with fork. Do a minimum of mixing. Do not worry if it looks marbled. Roll out and line a pie plate. Bake 7 minutes. Remove from oven, fill and bake for 1 hour at 350° F.

Filling
3 cups cooked pumpkin or squash
1/4 block soft tofu
1/4 cup arrowroot
1/2 cup rice syrup
1/4 cup almond butter
1 tsp vanilla
1 tsp cinnamon
1 tsp nutmeg
1/8 tsp ground cloves
1/2 cup maple syrup

In a food processor, mix filling until very smooth. Pour into partially baked pie shell. Bake for one hour at 350° F.

Serves 8-10

Pecan Crisp Cookies (gluten free)

2 cups rice flour
2 cups pecans, finely ground
2 tsp ground cinnamon
1 tsp ground cardamom
1 tsp salt
3/4 cup canola oil
3/4 cup maple syrup

Preheat oven to 350 degrees. Mix all the dry ingredients in one bowl.
Whisk oil and maple syrup together in a separate bowl. Pour the
liquid into the dry. Mix well with a spatula. It may seem wet at
first, but the rice flour will absorb the liquid gradually.
Use a spoon or an ice-cream scoop to place dough on a cookie sheet
which has either been oiled or lined with parchment paper.
Press the cookie dough with a wet fork until they are fairly thin.
Bake at 350 degrees for about 20 minutes, or until they are golden
brown and crisp.

Yield: about 2 dozen cookies.

Raisin Pie

Pie Crust
Use either the Rice Crust (page 146) or the Nut Crust (page 137)

Filling
1 cup organic Flame or Thompson raisins
1 cup warm water
1 litre (4 cups) vanilla soymilk
1/4 cup agar flakes
1/2 cup maple syrup
1/3 cup arrowroot flour
1 tsp vanilla extract

Soak raisins in water for one hour. Drain. Discard liquid. Set aside.

Bring soymilk and agar to a boil on medium heat. Reduce heat and simmer until agar is completely dissolved. Add drained raisins; return to a boil, reduce heat. Mix arrowroot into the maple syrup; whisk it into the simmering soymilk mixture until thick. It will thicken almost immediately. Remove from heat. Allow to cool for 15-30 minutes. Stir vanilla extract into soymilk mixture; pour into cooled pie shell. Allow to set in refrigerator for 2-3 hours.

Serves 8-10

Raspberry Pie

Pie Crust
1 Nut Crust (page 137)

Filling
4 cups raspberries, fresh or frozen
1/4 cup agar flakes
2 cups raspberry juice or apple juice
1/3 cup arrowroot
3/4-1 cup maple syrup

In a pot, place raspberry or apple juice and agar. Bring to a rolling boil on high heat, uncovered. As soon as the juice comes to a boil, turn heat to medium and cook for 2-3 minutes to entirely dissolve the agar. In a bowl, whisk arrowroot in maple syrup until fully dissolved. When agar is fully dissolved, pour the maple syrup-arrowroot mixture into the pot. Whisk until thick; this will take 1-2 minutes. Remove from heat, add raspberries and allow to cool. Pour into a cooled pie crust. Refrigerate for 1-2 hours, until set.

Serves 8-10

Raspberry Tofu Squares

Base
2 cups large flake rolled oats
1 cup almonds
pinch of salt
1/2 tsp cinnamon
2 cups barley, wheat or spelt flour
1/4 cup plus 1 tbsp corn oil
1/4 cup plus 1 tbsp maple syrup

Topping
1 block firm tofu
1/2 block soft tofu
1/2 cup cashew butter
1 tbsp vanilla
1 cup rice malt
1/4 cup maple syrup
1/4 cup tsp salt
3/4 cup arrowroot
4 cups raspberries
1/4 cup lemon juice

Line a 9 x 13 inch pan with parchment paper. Blend oats, almonds, salt and cinnamon in a food processor until finely ground. Turn out into a bowl, add barley flour and mix with a fork. Add oil and maple syrup. Mix then press evenly into the baking pan. Bake at 350° F for 10 minutes.

Reserve half of the raspberries. Process the remaining 2 cups with the rest of the filling ingredients until well blended. Fold the 2 cups of reserved raspberries into topping and pour over partially baked crust. Cook at 350° F for 30 minutes. Cool.

Makes 24 squares

Rice Pudding

1 cup sweet brown rice
3 cups water
3 cups apple juice
pinch of salt
1 litre soy milk
1/2 cup raisins
1/2 cup dried fruit, diced (apricots, peaches, apples)

Cook rice in water until very soft. Add apple juice and continue to cook for 1 hour. Place on a heat dispenser to avoid sticking. Keep at very low heat, stirring occasionally.

Add soy milk, raisins and dried fruit, and cook on low heat until the mixture boils. Take off heat and stir. Let sit for 1-2 hours.

Serves 12.

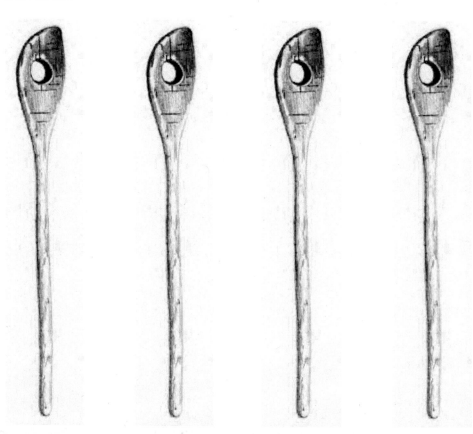

Seed Cookies

Dry Ingredients
2 cups large-flake rolled oats
1 cup spelt flour
3/4 cup sesame seeds
1 1/2 cups sunflower seeds
1/2 cup flax seeds
pinch of salt

Wet Ingredients
1/2 cup canola oil
1/2 cup rice malt
1/2 cup maple syrup
1/3 cup tahini
1 tbsp vanilla
1/2 cup apple juice

Mix dry ingredients together. Mix wet ingredients together. Combine wet and dry ingredients. Drop by tablespoon onto parchment paper lined cookie sheets and bake at 350° F for 30-35 minutes until light brown.

Makes 2 1/2 dozen cookies

Sesame Cookies

3 cups whole wheat pastry flour
1 cup sesame seeds (lightly roasted in oven: 350° F for 5 minutes)
1/8 tsp salt
1 tsp cinnamon
1 cup rice syrup
3/4 cup corn oil
2 tbsp maple syrup
1 tsp vanilla

In a bowl mix flour, sesame seeds, baking powder, salt and cinnamon. In a smaller bowl mix rice syrup, corn oil, maple syrup, and vanilla with a whisk to obtain a smooth mixture.

Pour wet mixture over dry ingredients and mix well.

On parchment paper lined cookie sheets, place large teaspoons of the mixture; flatten with wet hand. Keep a cup of water handy, in which to dip your hands.

Place cookie sheets in oven and bake at 350 F for 15-20 minutes or until brown at edges. Do not let cookies get too dark. They will be soft on coming out of the oven but will harden as they cool.

Do not place too close together on cookie sheets; they spread!

Makes 2 dozen cookies

Strawberry Cake With Strawberry Glaze

Dry Ingredients
4 1/2 cups spelt or soft wheat flour
3 tsp non-alum baking powder
pinch of salt

Wet Ingredients
1/2 cup corn oil
3/4 cup maple syrup
1 tsp vanilla
1 cup strawberries, washed and sliced
1 1/2 - 2 cups apple strawberry juice

Oil and flour a 10 inch tube pan. In one bowl stir the flour and baking powder well. In a second bowl mix all the wet ingredients together. Combine the wet and dry ingredients, mixing very well and quickly. Pour cake batter into prepared pan and bake at 350° F for 45 minutes to 1 hour until knife comes out clean. Let cool for 10 minutes in the pan. Turn out and let cool. Serve with strawberry sauce or fresh strawberries.

Glaze
2-4 cups fresh strawberries, washed and sliced
2 cups strawberry apple juice
1/4 cup maple syrup
2 tbsp arrowroot or kudzu

Bring the strawberry apple juice to the boil in a saucepan. Dissolve the arrowroot or kudzu in the maple syrup. Add to the boiling juice, which should immediately become thick and glossy. Take off heat and add the strawberries. Serve over the cake.

Other fruits can be used in place of the strawberries. Change the fruit juice to suit the chosen fruit. Apple juice goes with everything.

Serves 8-10

Strawberry Shortcake

2 cups soft whole wheat flour
2 tsp baking powder
pinch of salt
1/2 cup maple syrup
1/4 cup melted butter *or* cold-pressed corn oil
1/2 cup soy milk
1 tsp vanilla

Place flour, baking powder and salt in bowl. In another bowl mix wet ingredients. Combine wet and dry ingredients, mixing well. Pour into a 9 x 9 inch oiled and floured pan. Bake at 350° F for 20-30 minutes. Allow to cool. When cold, top with 2 cups whipped cream and 4 cups washed and sliced strawberries.

Teff Almond Cookies

Dry Ingredients
2 cups rolled oats (large-flake, slow cooking)
2 cups teff flour
2 cups almonds
1/4 tsp freshly grated nutmeg
pinch of salt

Wet Ingredients
2/3 cup canola oil
2/3 cup maple syrup
2 tsp vanilla
1/3 cup orange juice
2 tsp orange rind

In a food processor, grind oats and almonds to a fine breadcrumb consistency.

Place into a bowl. Add flour, nutmeg, and salt. Stir to mix.

In another bowl, mix oil, syrup, vanilla, orange juice, and rind.

Pour wet ingredients over dry; combine well.

Drop big spoonfuls onto a cookie sheet. Flatten with a fork dipped in water. Bake at 325° F for 20-25 minutes, until lightly browned.

Cool on a rack.

Makes 2 dozen cookies

Three Fruit Pie

Wheat-Free Crust
1 cup spelt flour
1 cup barley flour
1/2 tsp of salt
1/2 cup corn oil (cold pressed, unrefined)
1/2-1/3 cup cold water

Filling
4 cups apples, thinly sliced
2 cups other fruit, i.e.: rhubarb, pears, strawberries, blueberries or
   mixture (slice large fruit; leave small fruit whole)
1/2 cup Thompson raisins (organic)
1/2 cup sucanat (unrefined cane sugar; optional)
1/4 cup arrowroot flour

Topping
1 1/2 cups finely chopped almonds, walnuts or pecans
3 tbsp rice syrup

Place flour in bowl. Stir in salt with a fork. Add oil alternately with the water, and continue to mix gently until all flour is mixed in. (Take care not to over mix.) Roll out on waxed paper and place into pie plate. In a bowl, mix all ingredients for filling thoroughly. Place in unbaked pie shell.

Mix nuts and rice syrup (it will be very sticky). With wet hands flatten small amounts and cover top of pie all over. Place in a pre-heated oven at 325-350° F and bake for 1-1 1/4 hours until top is golden and fruit is cooked (topping becomes crisp as it has no flour in it).

Serves 8

Thumbprint Cookies

2 cups old fashioned large oat flakes
2 cups pecans or walnuts
2 cups whole wheat soft pastry flour
pinch of salt
1 tsp cinnamon
1 tsp nutmeg
2/3 cup maple syrup
2/3 cup corn oil
1/2 cup orange juice (fresh squeezed)
1 tsp orange rind
2 tsp vanilla

In a food processor, grind oats until fine. Add pecans or walnuts and process until nuts are coarsely ground. Place in a bowl and add flour, salt and spices. In a smaller bowl mix maple syrup, oil, orange juice, orange rind and vanilla. Mix quickly but thoroughly, wet into dry. Drop spoonfuls of mix onto oiled cookie sheets, flatten with fork dipped in water. In the centre of each cookie make a depression with thumb or forefinger and fill with jam or unsweetened apple butter. Bake at 350° F for 20-25 minutes.

Makes 24-30 large cookies.

Tofu Mocha Pie

Pie Crust
see pages 133 and 141 for pie crusts

Filling
4 cups apple juice
1/3 cup agar flakes
1/2 block soft tofu (1 cup)
1/2 cup cashew butter
1/2 cup carob powder
1/3 cup grain coffee powder
2 tbsp vanilla
1/3 cup arrowroot
3/4 cup maple syrup

In a saucepan bring 2 cups apple juice and agar flakes to a boil until agar has dissolved.

In a blender, mix the tofu, cashew butter, carob powder, grain coffee, vanilla and the remaining 2 cups of apple juice. Add to the saucepan and bring the mixture to a boil.

Dissolve the arrowroot in the maple syrup and add to the boiling mixture. Stir for 1 minute. The mixture will begin to thicken. Turn off the heat and cool. When cooled, pour into pie crust and refrigerate until fully set and chilled.

Trifle

Custard
2 cups vanilla soy milk
2 tbsp agar flakes
2 tbsp arrowroot
1/3 cup maple syrup

Bring soy milk and agar to a boil on low heat. Cook for 2-3 minutes until agar is completely dissolved. Stir arrowroot into maple syrup and mix thoroughly. Add to boiling soy milk and stir for 1 minute until thick. Take off heat and set aside.

Cake
2 cups any kind of cake or cookies
2-4 medium bananas
1-2 cups raspberries, strawberries, blackberries, and/or sliced kiwis or other soft fruit

In a 3 litre glass bowl, place layers
1. half of the cake, crumbled
2. two sliced bananas
3. soft fruit or fruit preserves
4. custard

Repeat the four layers. Refrigerate for 2-3 hours. Serve garnished with sliced berries or other fruit.

Serves 8-10

Unsweetened Apple Pie

Wheat Crust
3 cups soft, whole wheat pastry flour
3/4 cup corn oil
3/4 cup chilled water
a pinch of salt

Filling
6-8 cups cored apples, thinly sliced
pinch of freshly grated nutmeg and/or cinnamon to taste

Place flour and salt in a large mixing bowl, using a fork to combine. Stirring gently, alternately pour portions of corn oil and water over flour until it forms a ball of dough. Do not over-work flour combination beyond this point. Mixture should be of a soft consistency. Do not worry if flour appears to be 'marbled' and unmixed - this will work itself out in rolling.

On a sheet of waxed paper, lightly sprinkle with flour and roll out slightly more than half of the dough mixture to 1/8 inch thick. Carefully drape rolled dough onto pie plate. Fill with sliced apples and add desired spices. Roll out remaining dough to same thickness and cover sliced apples. Pinch edges with fingers to seal dough together. Trim around the pie plate edge with a fork or knife. Prick and/or slash dough shell on top, to allow the steam to escape. Bake in preheated 350° F oven for 45 - 60 minutes.

Makes 8 large pieces

Variation: for a wheat-free crust, use:
1 1/2 cups spelt flour
1/2 cup barley flour
pinch of salt
7/8 cup corn or canola oil
3/4-7/8 cup water or unsweetened fruit juice

Upside Down Cake

Base
4-5 cups thinly sliced apples or pears
1/4 cup fruit juice
1/4 cup maple syrup
1 tbsp arrowroot
1/4 cup raspberry or apple juice

In a pot, cook the apples with 1/4 cup fruit juice. Cover and cook until the apples are semi-soft but not mushy. Dissolve the 1 tbsp of arrowroot in the raspberry or apple juice, add to the apple mixture along with the maple syrup. Cook until thick (1-2 minutes). Turn off heat. Pour into a 9 x 9 inch glass baking pan.

Cake

Dry Ingredients
3 cups flour
2 tsp non-alum baking powder

Wet Ingredients
1/2 cup corn oil
1/2 cup maple syrup
3/4 cup juice or soy milk
1 tbsp vanilla

In a bowl, mix flour and baking powder. Mix wet ingredients in a separate bowl. Add wet to dry. Mix well and pour cake batter over fruit. Bake at 350° F for 45-55 minutes. Serve upside down.

Serves 8-10

Vegetarian Mincemeat

5 cups grated apples
4 cups currants
4 cups sultanas or other raisins
4 cups Thompson raisins
1 cup chopped crystallized orange and lemon peel
the juice and grated rind of 4 lemons
1 cup brandy
2 tsp ground cinnamon
1/2 tsp ground mace
1/2 tsp ground nutmeg

Place currants, sultanas and raisins in a large bowl. Cover with boiling water. Let stand 5 minutes. Drain in colander. Return to bowl. Add grated apples, peel, lemon rind, lemon juice, spices. Add brandy. Mix well.
Pack tightly into jars, cover and let sit in cold storage or refrigeration for 3 to 4 weeks before using.

Yield: filling for 3 eight inch pies.

Note: to crystallize orange and lemon peel: save the peel of organic oranges and lemons. Place them in a pot. Cover with cold water. Bring to a boil and continue to boil for 5 minutes. Drain. Rinse in cold water. Drain again. Place the peels back in the pot with maple syrup (1 cup of maple syrup for 5 to 6 cups of peel). Cook on low heat until soft, 30 to 40 minutes.

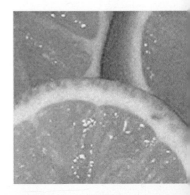

SOURDOUGH BREAD

To start you need starter;
to finish you need time.

Where to find the starter? It's out there, circulating in continual regeneration. Either someone will give you some, or you'll make your own. It's been 25 years since Helen gave me a few tablespoons; it was already old then. For fun, I have made others as well, but abandoned them and kept the original because of its superior qualities.

If no one gives you some, make your own. Mix about 1/2 cup of freshly milled organic whole grain flour with a cup of water. Let this sit, uncovered, in your kitchen. Due to the ambient temperature and whatever wild organisms that inhabit your kitchen, this flour/water mixture will begin to bubble, liquify, and smell after a few days. The smell should be of a clean, fermented, sour nature. Your starter has arrived! Transfer it to a glass jar, with the lid in place but not overly tightened. Keep it in the refrigerator.

There are any number of different breads; the variables are: ingredients, their proportions, and methodology. The variations in methodology can include both handling and baking techniques. I'll give you one way to make sourdough bread at home, with glimpses into other possibilities.

Start with well cooked brown rice. Instead of the usual 2 to 1 water to rice ratio, make it 4 or 5 to 1. The rice will be very well expanded. You could use leftover rice; re-cook it with more water. Leftover oatmeal porridge is another possibility (or millet, or corn-meal, etc.). Let this rice cool to approximately body temperature, or just slightly warmer. You can determine this range by simply sticking your finger into it. No fancy tools required.

At the restaurant, we soak overnight a mixture of sweet brown rice and either whole oats or whole rye berries (the former is used for spelt bread, the latter for rye). The following morning, after rinsing then replacing the water, we pressure-cook these for 1 1/2 hours. Removed from the stove, these pots sit until evening, by which time the well-cooked whole grains have swelled fully and cooled to room temperature. At home a pressure-cooker is not necessary.

The next step is to put together the sponge. Empty the pot of well-cooked grain into a large bowl. With a wooden spoon, mix in enough flour (we use either spelt or rye), so that it becomes the texture of a thick cake batter. To the spelt bread we add some whole flax seed. How much?, enough for visual and textural interest; you're not making flax bread, so not a lot. One more thing to add at this point: the starter. Put it all in, don't hold any back. Mix it in well. Cover the bowl with a clean towel or apron. This is to prevent anything from falling into your sponge, especially any wild yeasts floating in your space that could contaminate your starter. You are using a particular group of organisms to raise your bread.

Depending on the season and the temperature of your kitchen, you will choose a spot to let this covered bowl sit for the next 6 to 12 hours. There is a temperature range that the starter needs for optimum growing conditions. In the summer, let it sit on the counter. If your house is cold in the winter, consider placing it inside your turned off oven, or into your oven which has been slightly warmed, then turned off.

When you return to it, the sponge will be more liquid, and some bubbles will probably have formed. Again, you may detect a clean, fermented, sour smell. The whole sponge has turned into starter.

Add enough flour to your sponge to bring it back to the thick cake batter texture in which you had left it. Remove some starter for your next batch of bread. I use a one liter wide-mouthed glass mason jar, or you could use a tupperware type lidded canister. About half-full, return it to the refrigerator.

Only two more ingredients: flour and salt. Sprinkle the sponge surface with flour. Sprinkle salt on top of that: one generous teaspoon per loaf. The salt strengthens the gluten (helping the loaf to rise and stay risen), and rounds out the flavour. We remove the starter prior to adding the salt; you don't want the starter to become salty over time, and the wild yeasts and the salt don't really get along. If you forget to remove the starter until after you have added the salt, it's not the end of the world. You can even forget to reserve your starter up until your loaves are baking in the oven. Past that point, it is the end of the world (for your starter).

Once the salt has been stirred in, the balance of the flour is added, bit by bit. Mix in enough flour so that you can turn the dough out onto a floured board or counter-top. Scrape out the bowl with the wooden spoon. All those little bits will melt into the ball of dough.

It's now time for kneading. If you have added too much flour, it will feel dry and tough. Too little, it will be wet and sticky. Too dry, and your final loaves won't rise well, be heavy dense bricks. Too wet, they will rise, but then fall, flat and brick-like again.

Kneading. On a floured surface, gather the dough together into one mass. Using the heels of your floured hands, push down and away. Stop. Rotate the dough 90 degrees counter-clockwise. Reach under, lift the edge toward you (don't lift the whole ball), with the effect of re-gathering the dough into a tighter, closer mass. Again, with the heels of your hands, push down and away. You're not pushing down so hard as to break the surface of the dough. It's sticky in there; your hands would soon be covered. Rather, push down and along, so that the dough mass moves in a path away from you. Rotate 90 degrees counter-clockwise. Lift the farther edge back toward you and into itself. And so on. Repeat with attention and rythm, noticing the development of the gluten as it becomes more elastic. You will have to occasionally dust the counter and the top surface of the dough with flour to prevent it from becoming sticky. With practice, it only takes a few minutes to complete this kneading. You'll have in front of you, centred in a dusting of flour, a tight round mound of dough that springs back when lightly pressed with your fingers.

Let the dough rest for between 15 and 30 minutes. You will see that it rises during this time. The sourdough is developing and stretching the gluten. The bread dough is kneading itself. I find that if you insert a 20 minute resting period at one or two places earlier in the process (before adding the total quantity of flour), the final result will be a lighter loaf with superior texture.

Divide the dough into loaves. Knead each individual piece. Shape, and place in an oiled bread pan. This bread will be relatively heavy, so choose a loaf pan on the narrow and short side that will produce a loaf that is visually appealing. The final shaping can be frustrating. As with many details of bread making, it is easier learned through demonstration. But if you find yourself tackling it on your own, persevere in a relaxed and attentive manner.

Score the top of each loaf with a sharp knife using 2 or 3 diagonal slashes. This allows the heat to easier penetrate, and looks great. Let rise, away from drafts, in a warmish place (again, the turned off oven can work). When risen (between 45 minutes and 1 1/2 hours), bake in a pre-heated 350 degree oven for one hour. This can vary according to your oven and your loaf size.Remove from the pans immediately when done. It should look done on all sides, and give a hollow sound when tapped on its underside. Let cool on a rack. Don't put loaves into plastic until completely cooled, otherwise they will sweat.

Our rye bread takes a different turn after the salt has been added. Because of its low gluten content and sticky nature, it is a very different matter to turn out and knead a mound of rye dough. We don't. Instead, we mix rye flour into the sponge until it is difficult to add more. The dough at this point is moist and very stiff. We spoon it into oiled loaf pans. Using a large metal spoon, dipped in water, we shape the malleable dough into a pleasing loaf-like shape, cresting high in the centre. It then rises and is baked.

The number of loaves you'll make depends on the amount of grain and water with which you begin. I suggest you start with one cup or 1 1/4 cups of uncooked brown rice. From your own experience you'll soon develop quantities that suit you. This bread both keeps and freezes well.

The jar of sourdough starter that now lives in your refrigerator needs very little care, just to be fed occasionally. You are feeding it every time you use it to make bread. Every day is fine, as we do in the restaurant. So is once a week, or every second week. If you don't use it for a few weeks, you can feed it by stirring in a little flour (and water if it's too thick). If you forget it in the back of the fridge only to discover much later that it has a black liquid floating on top, even then you can revive it. Pour off the black liquid, add more flour and water; let it sit out of the cold of the refrigerator for several hours.

It is not very time consuming to make this bread. It takes a few short periods spread out in intervals over 24 hours or so. Enjoy.